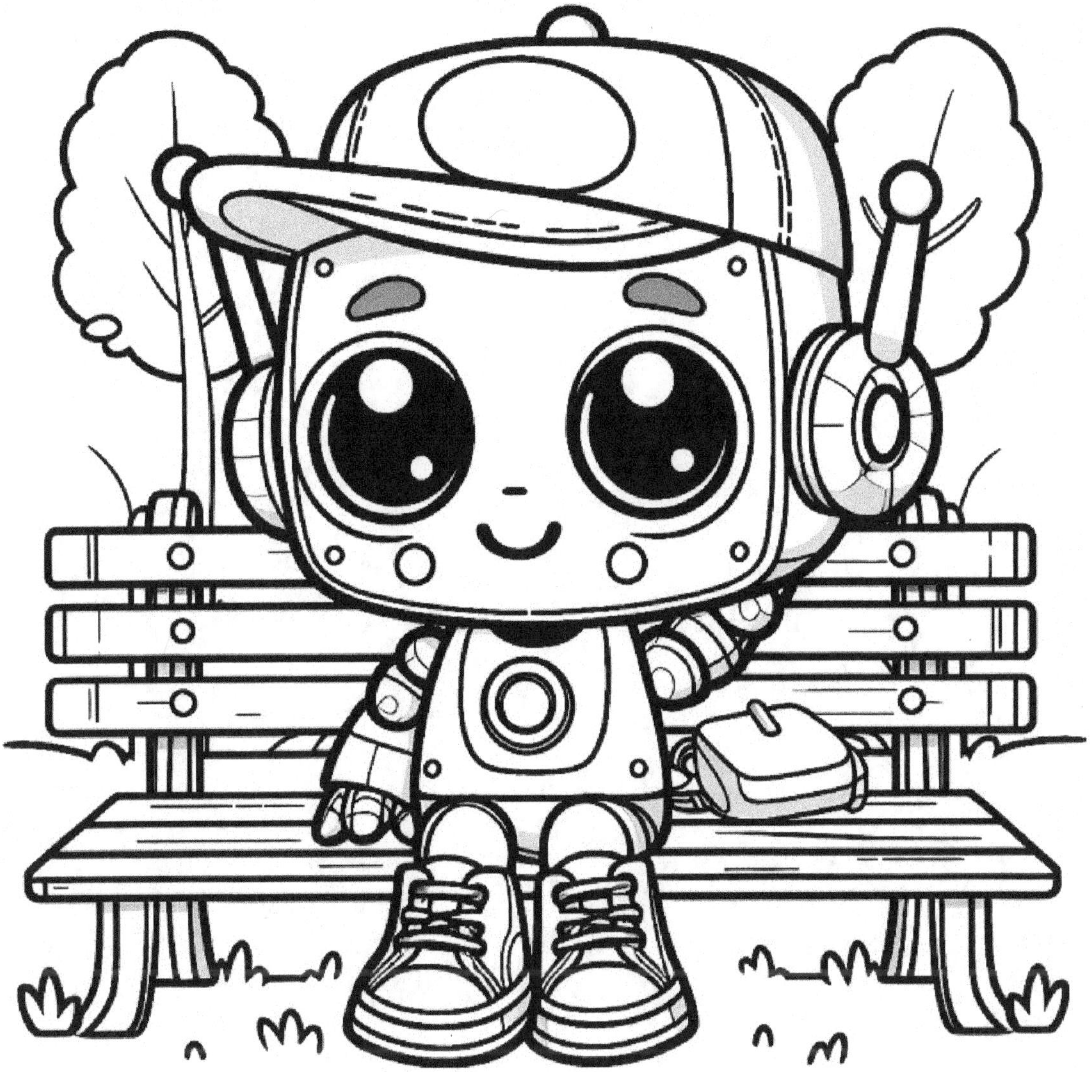

Hello, I'm Niti Liky, do you want to be my friend?

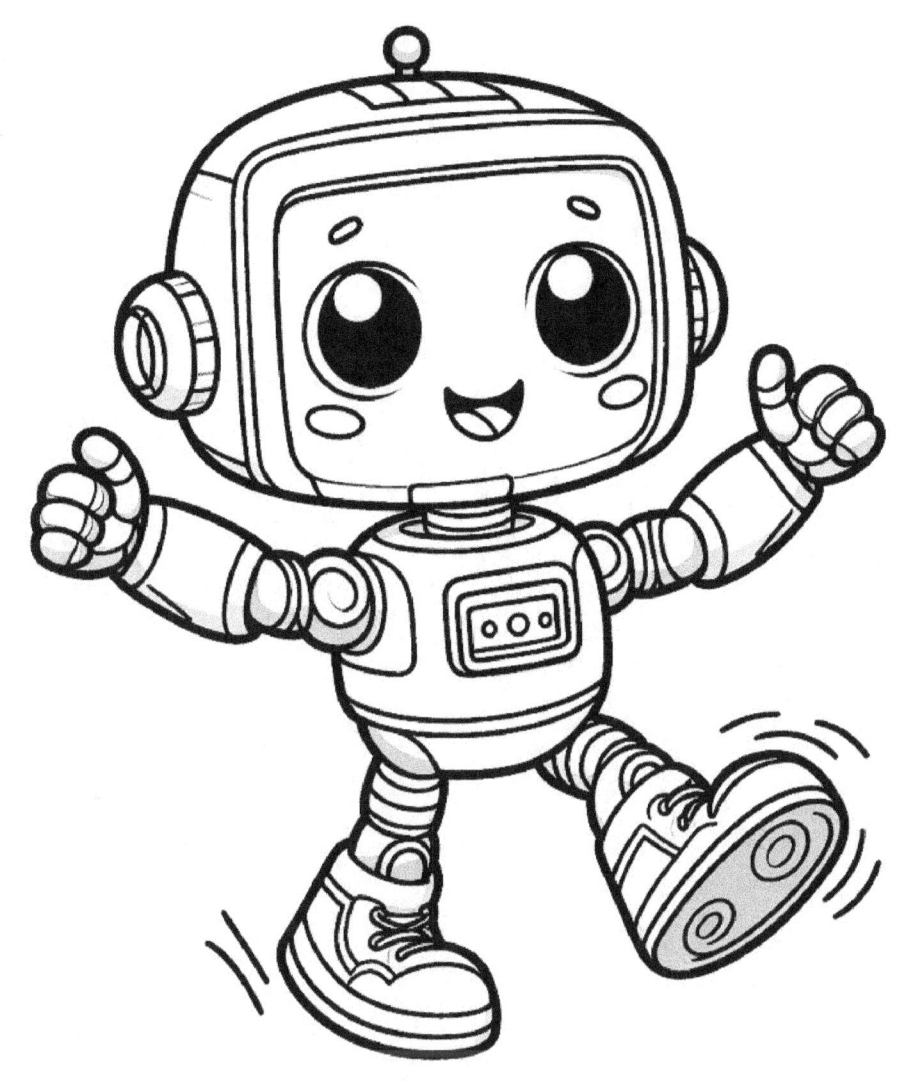

"Little Robot Niti Liky is a happy little robot
who lives in the city of robots.
He is very kind and loves to make friends!"

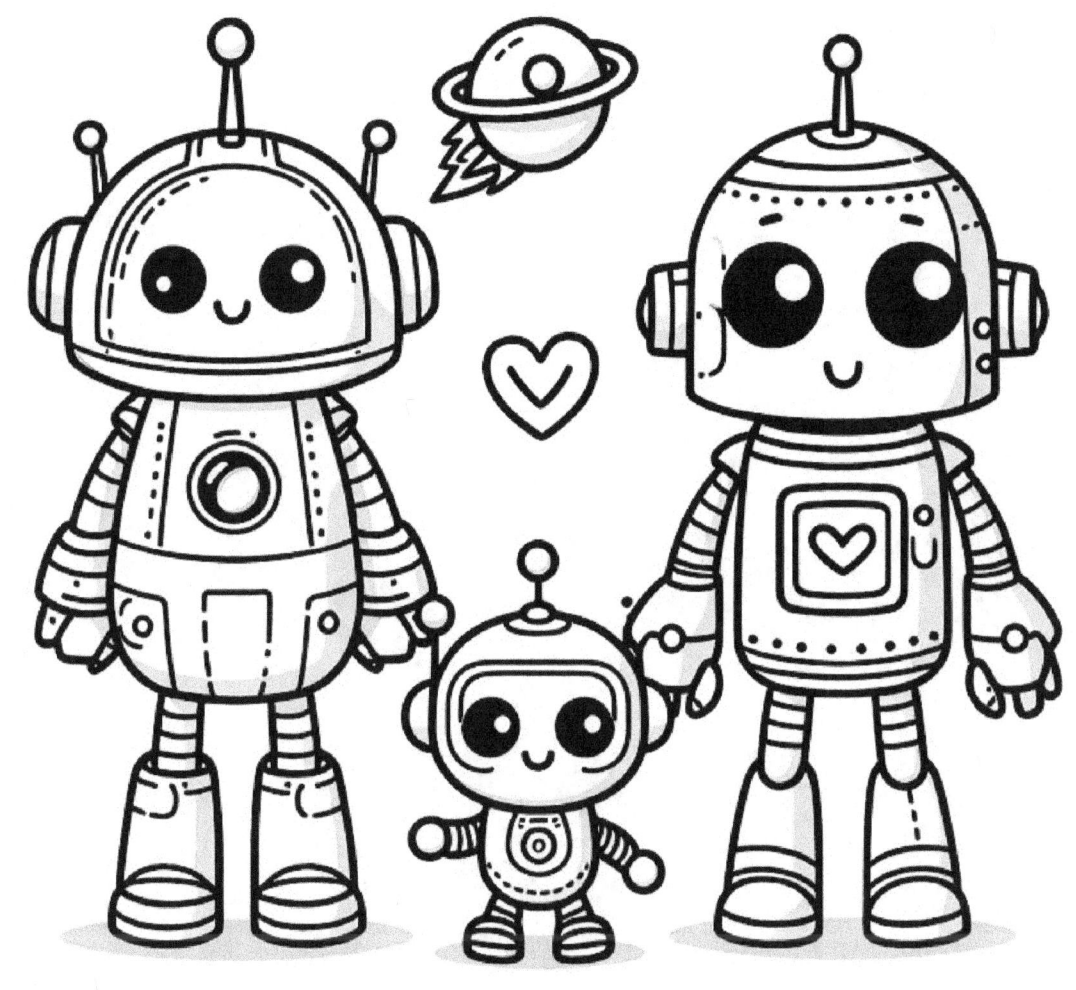

Niti Liky had a beautiful family: his father Robô Neti and his mother robô Mille.

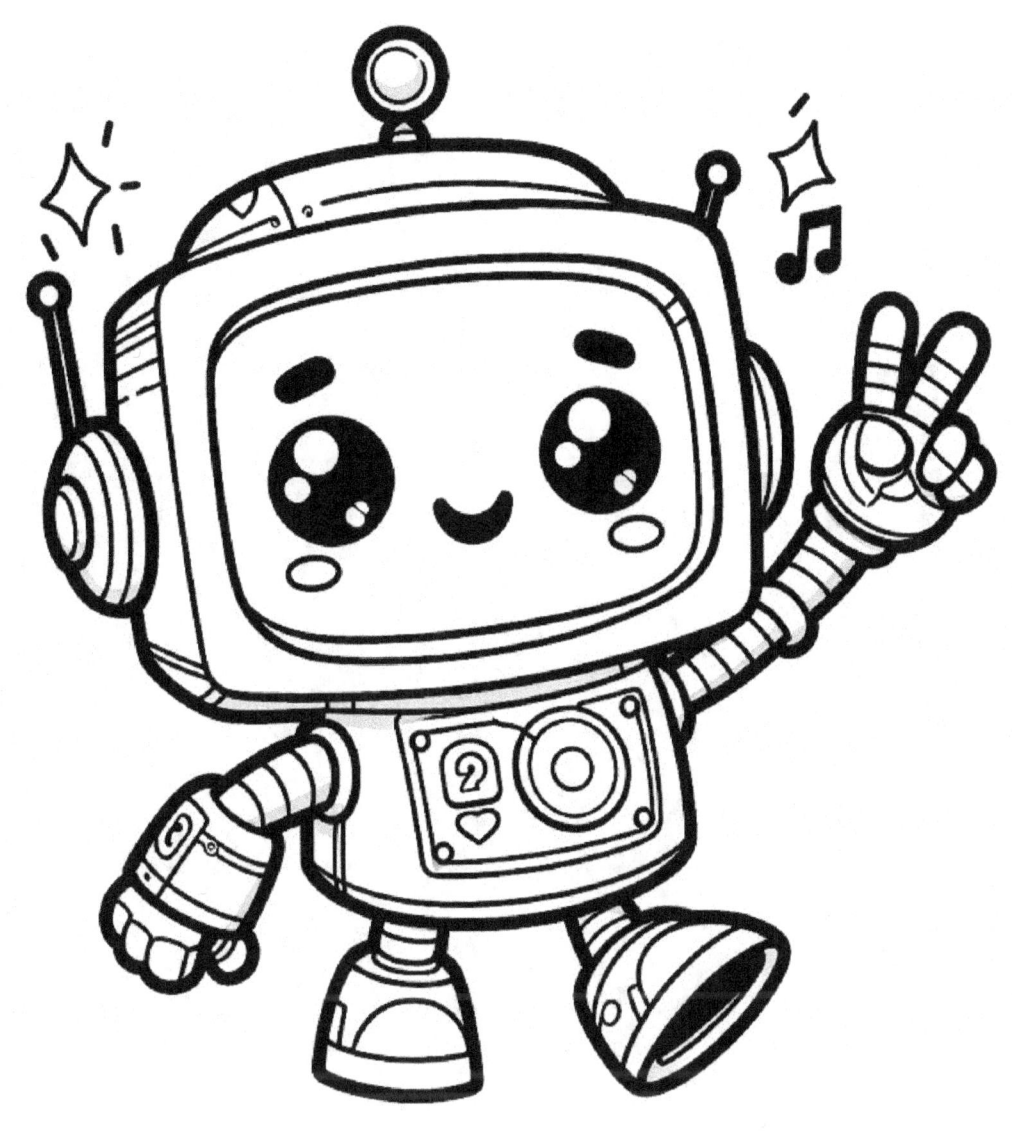

His favorite hobby was dancing.

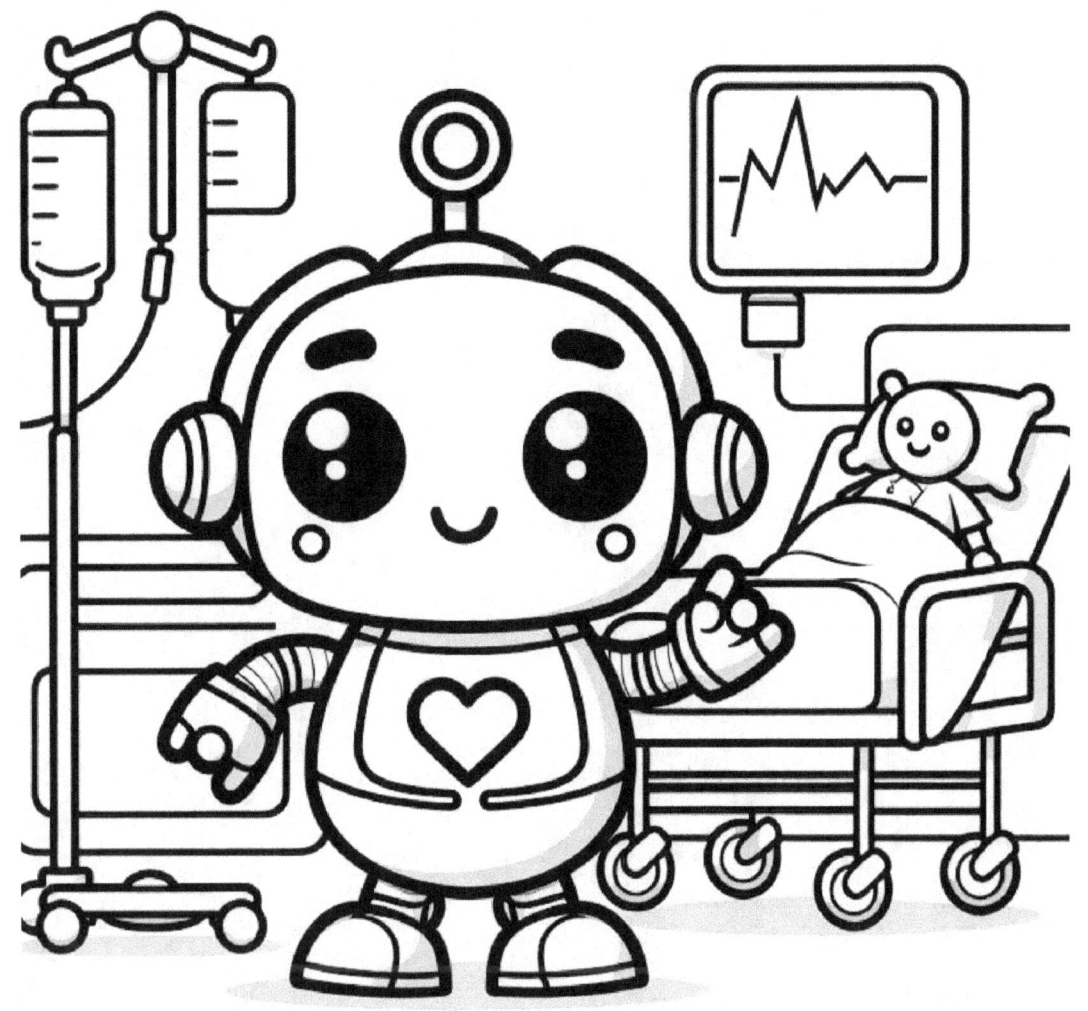

One thing he hates is being sick.

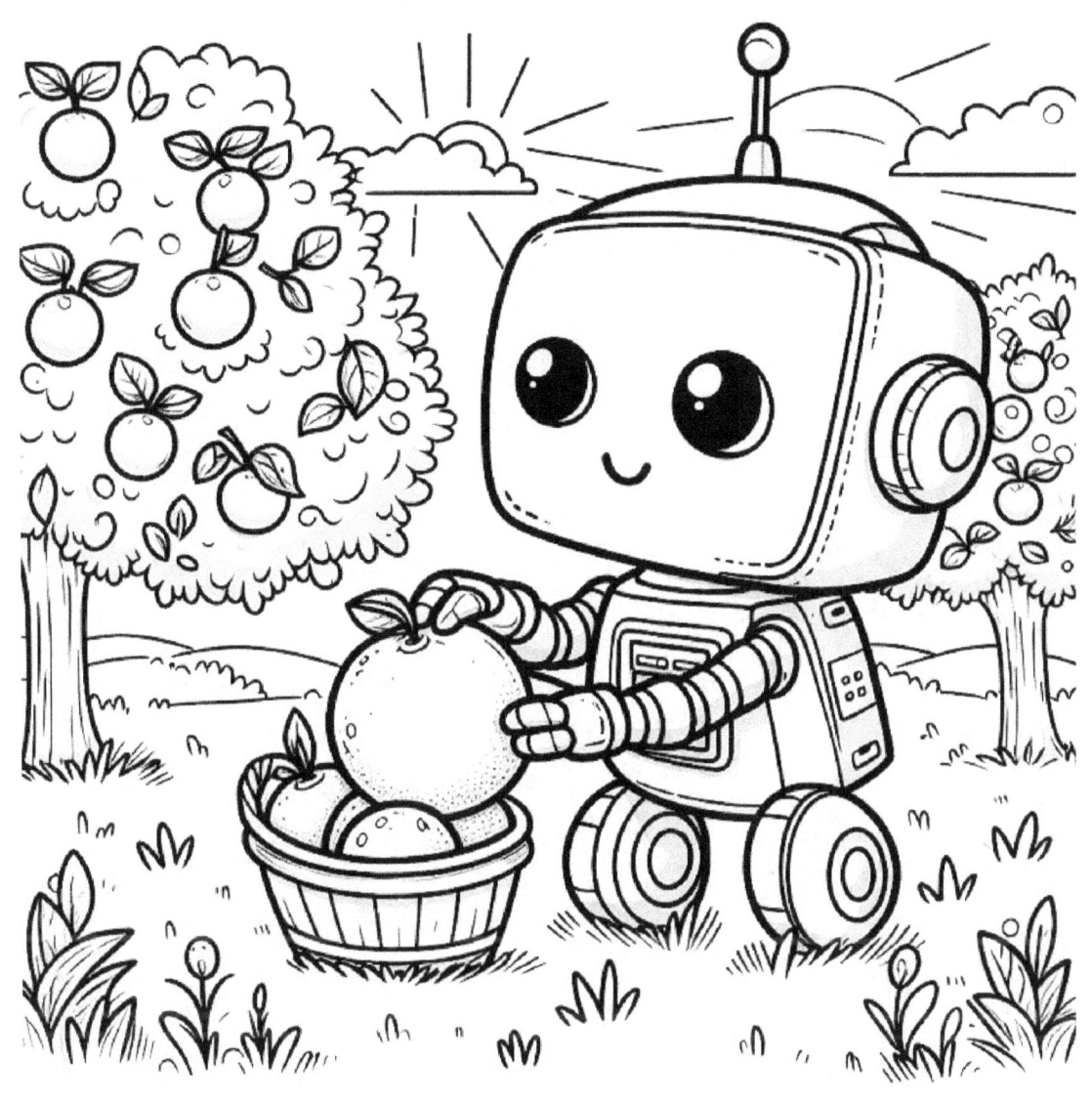

Every morning, he loved to pick fruits from
his orchard.

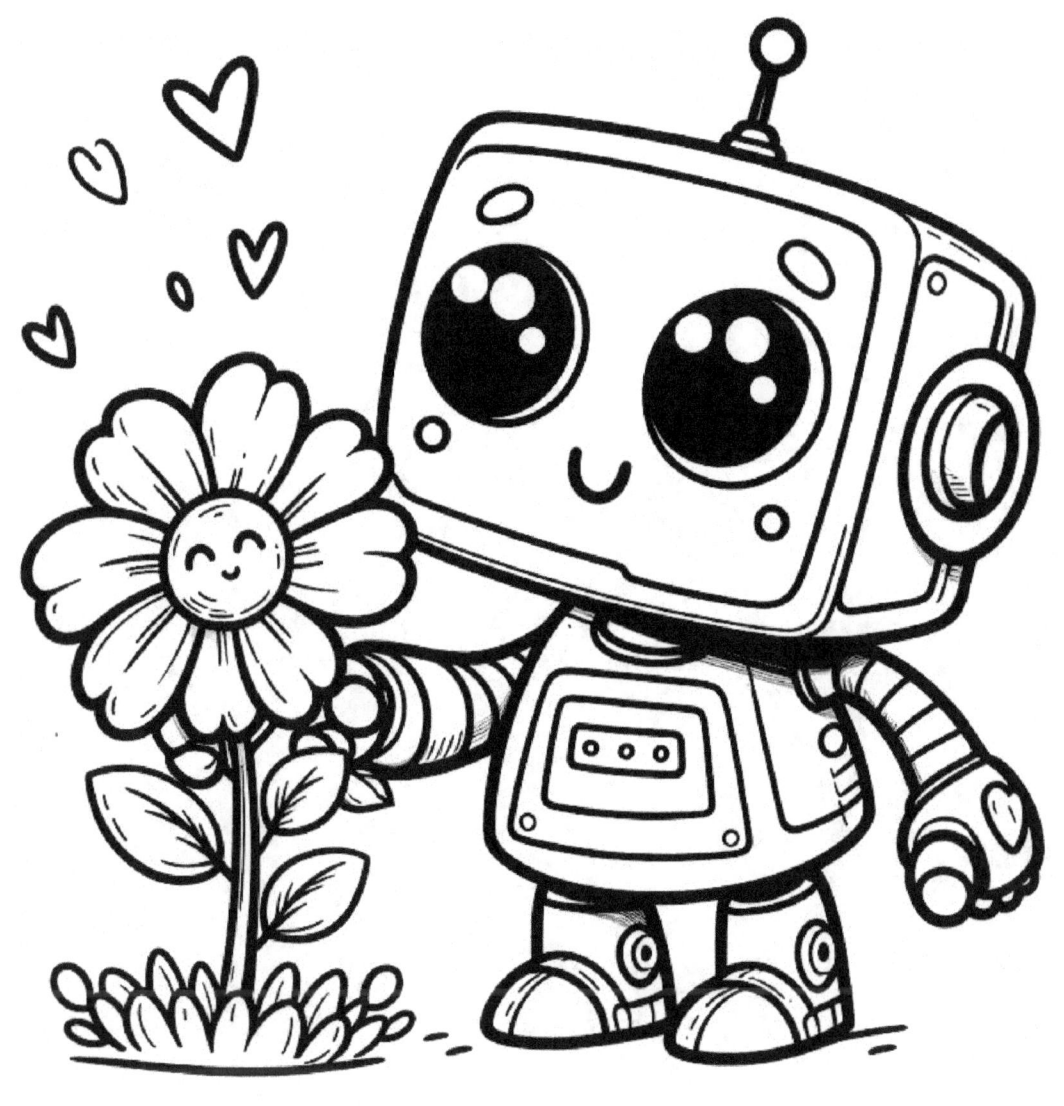

And before leaving, he would go to the garden to see its beautiful flowers.

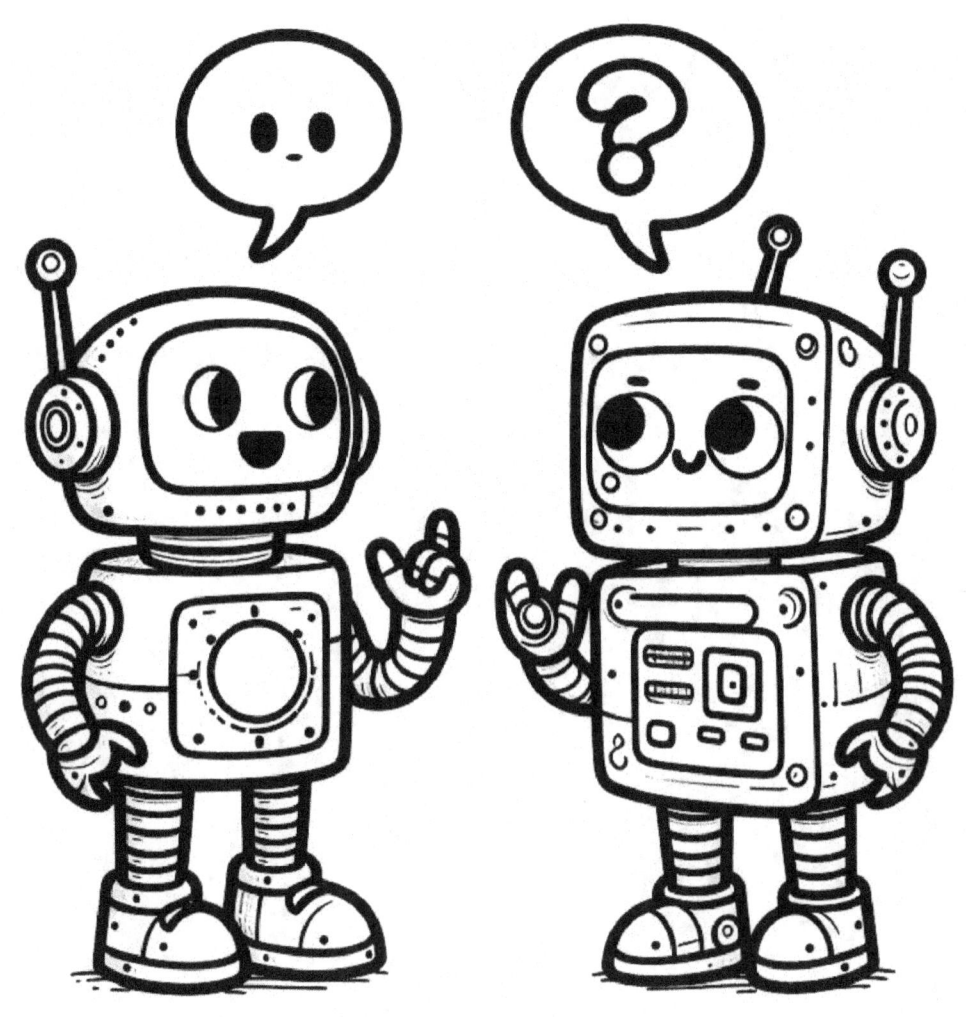

His best friend was Dylan.

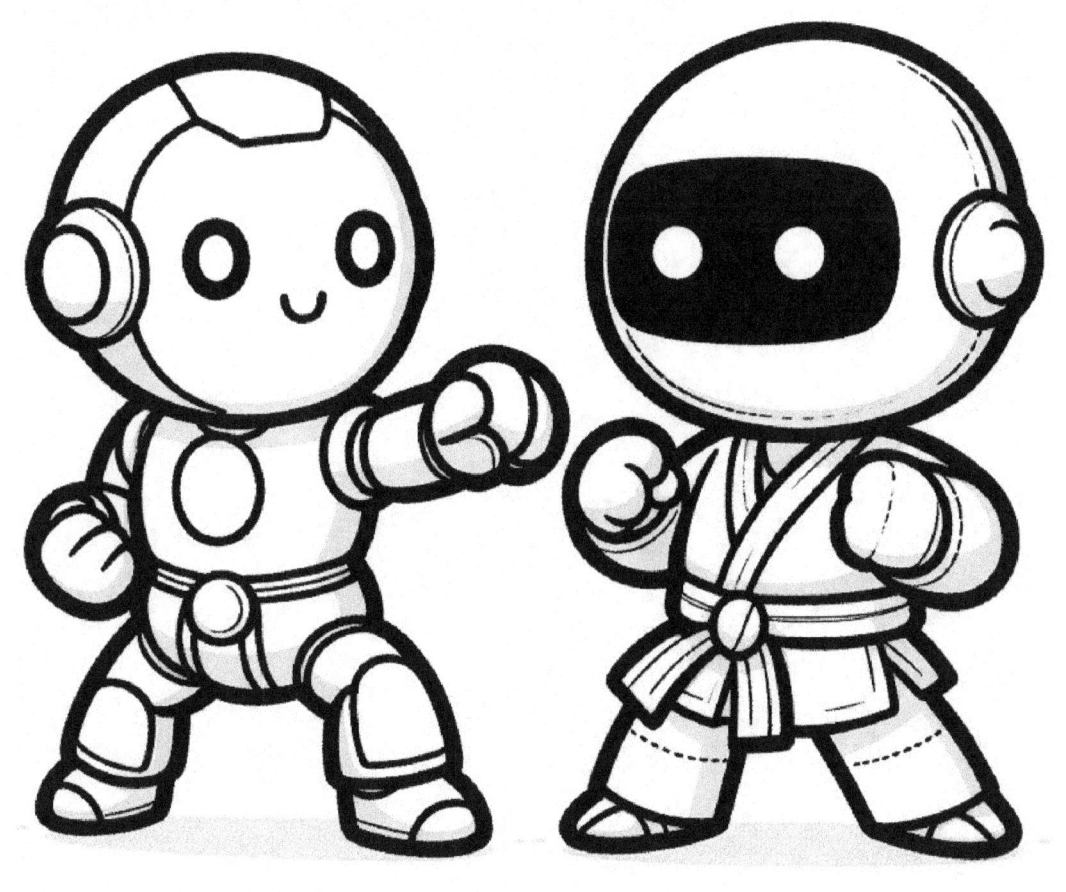

Both were training karate to compete in the international robot championship.

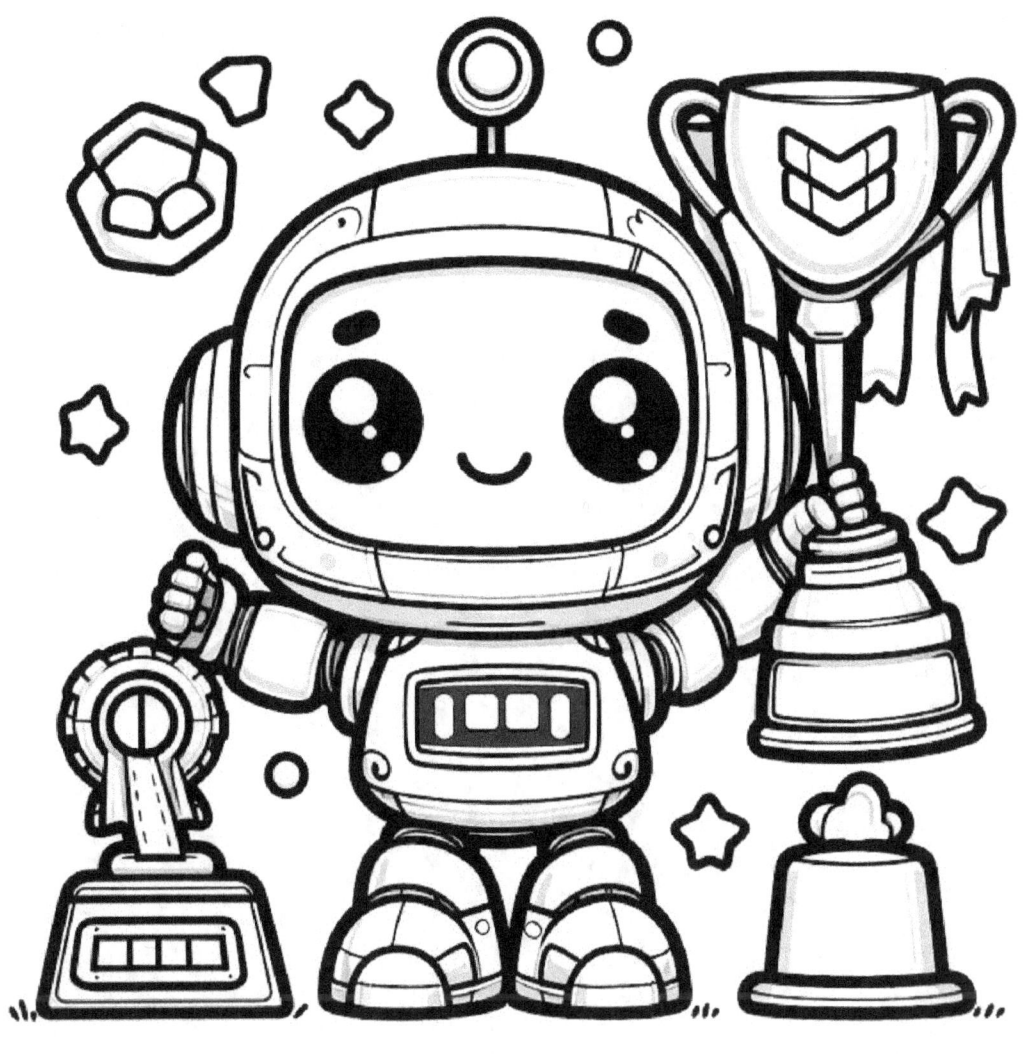

All his effort paid off because in the international robot championship, Nitti Liky ranked among the top 3.

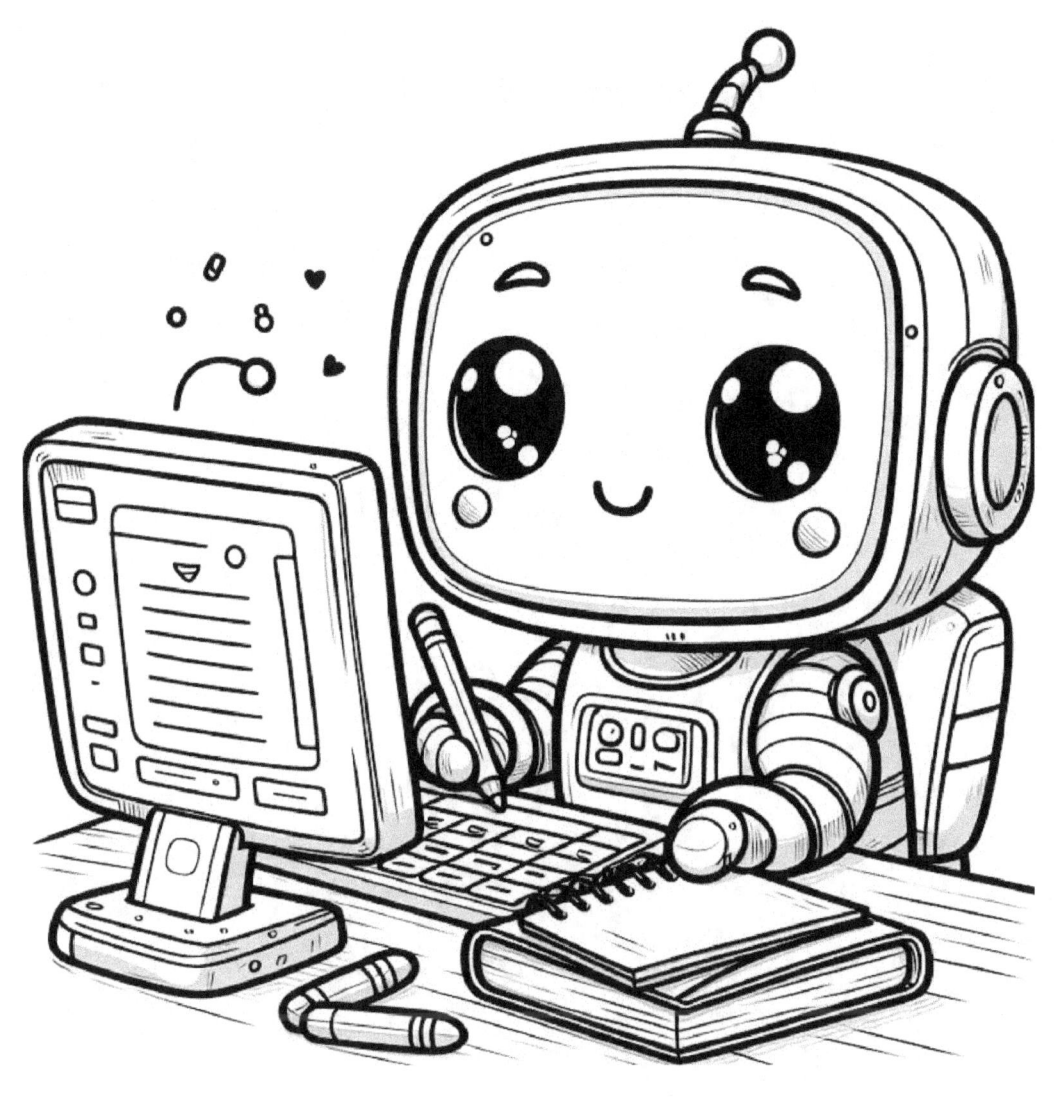

Niti Liky never neglected his studies; he was an exemplary student.

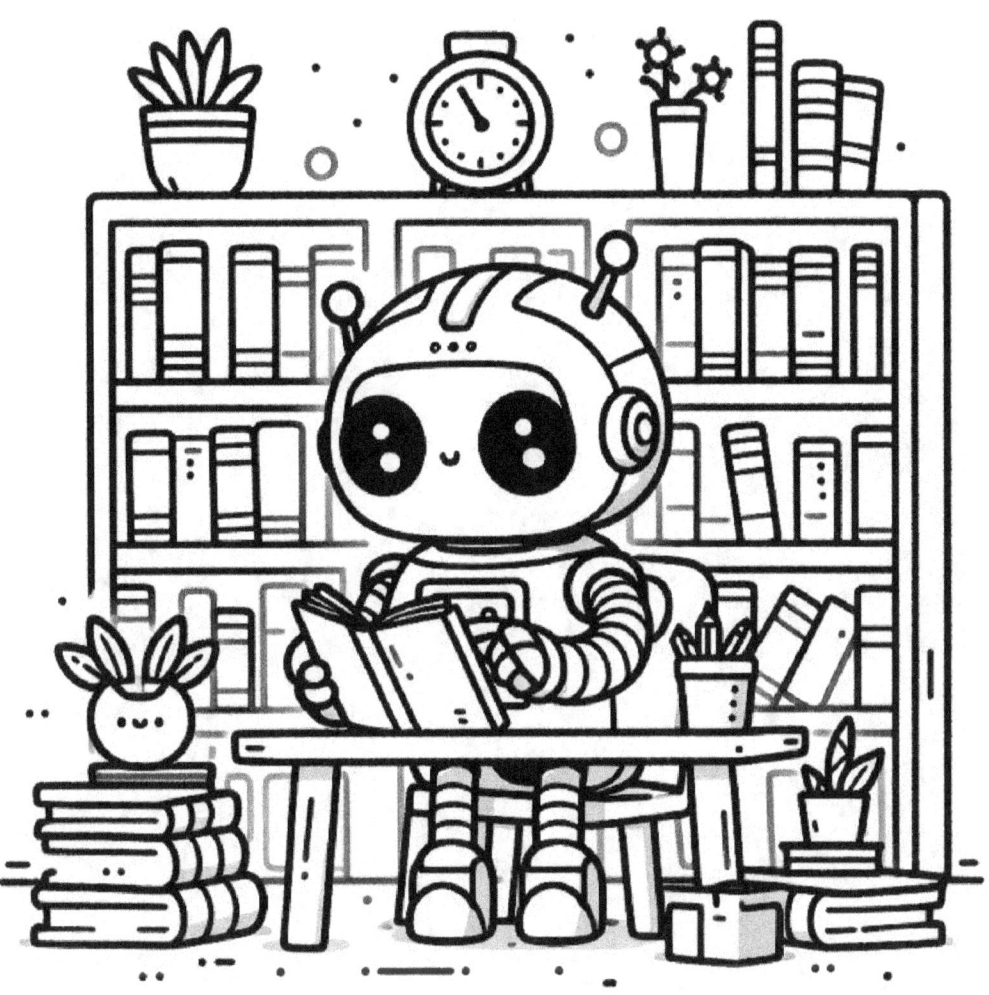

He dedicated many hours of his day to becoming a robot doctor.

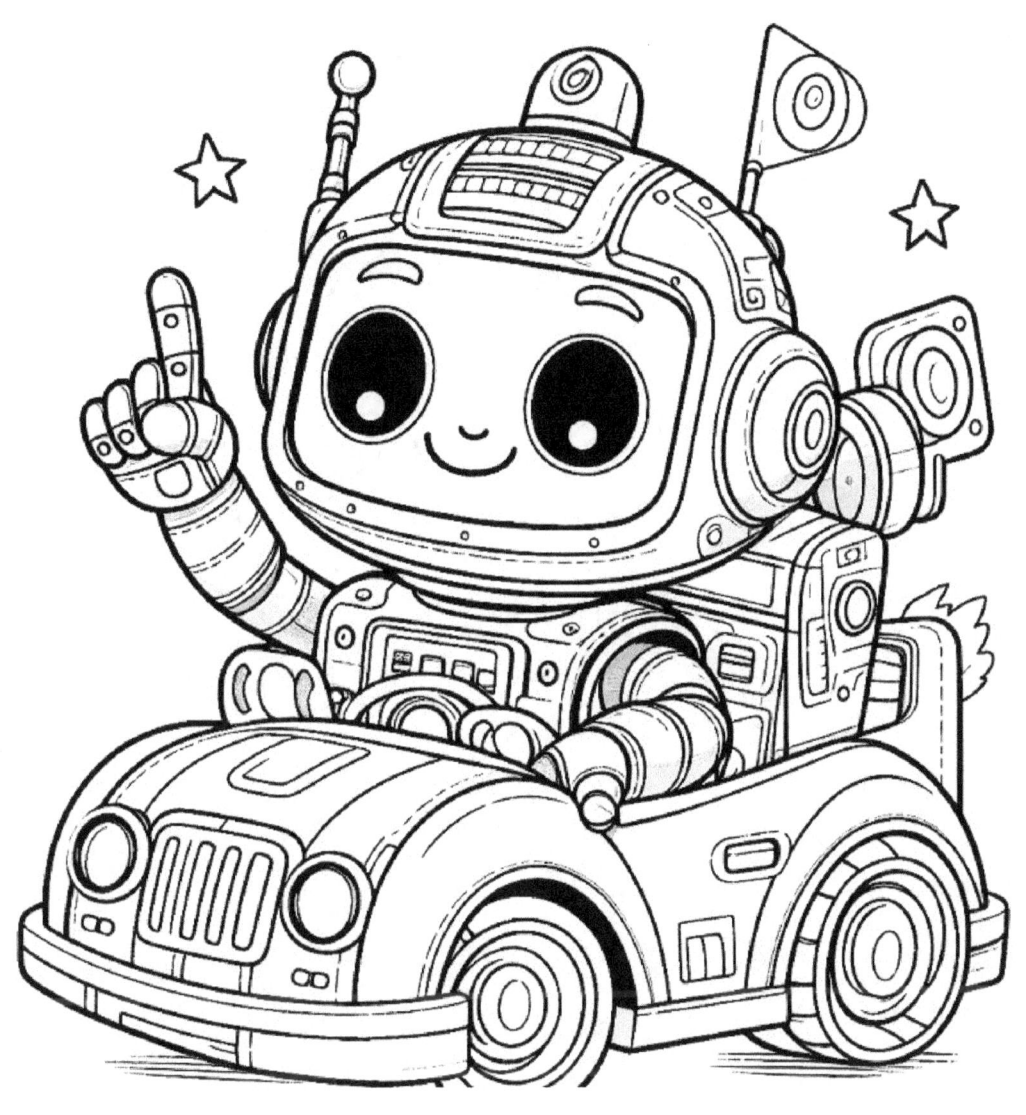

On his way to school, he noticed a strange noise in his car.

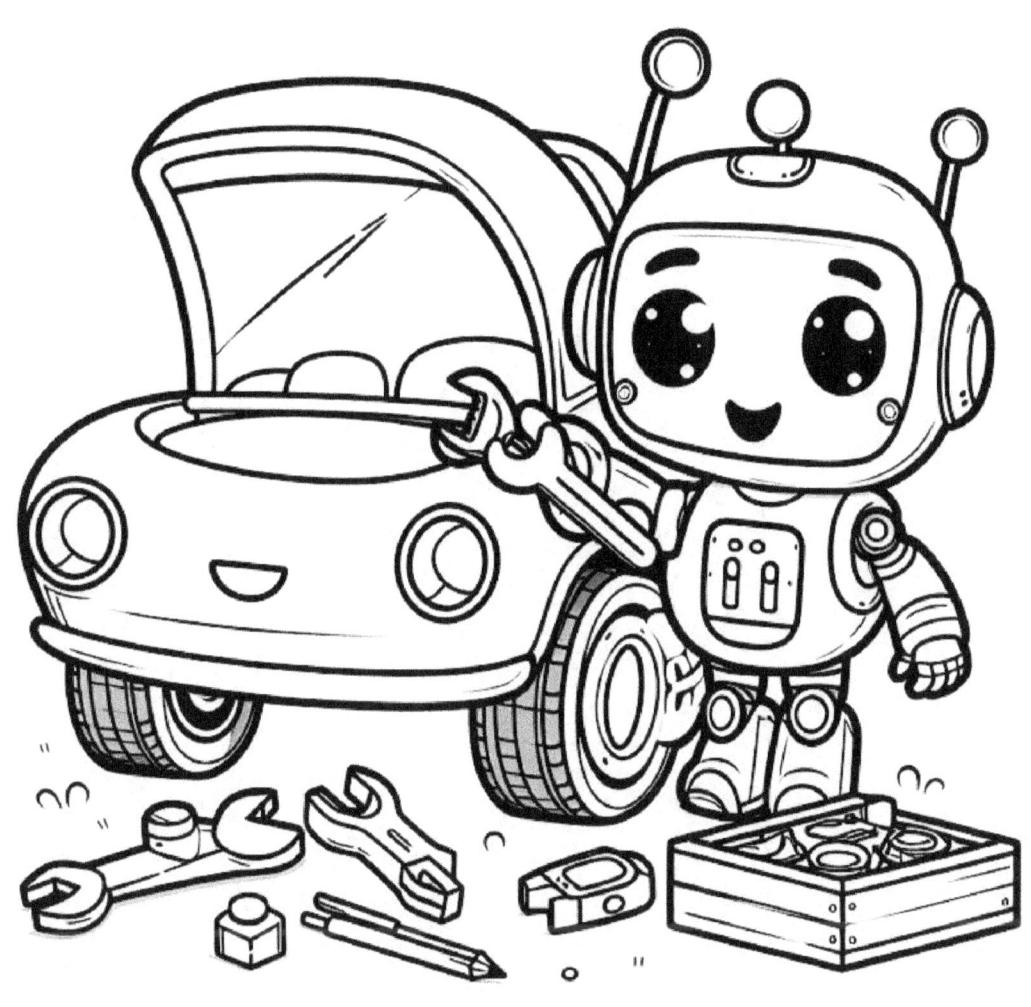

One day, his car broke down,
and Niti Liky had to fix it.

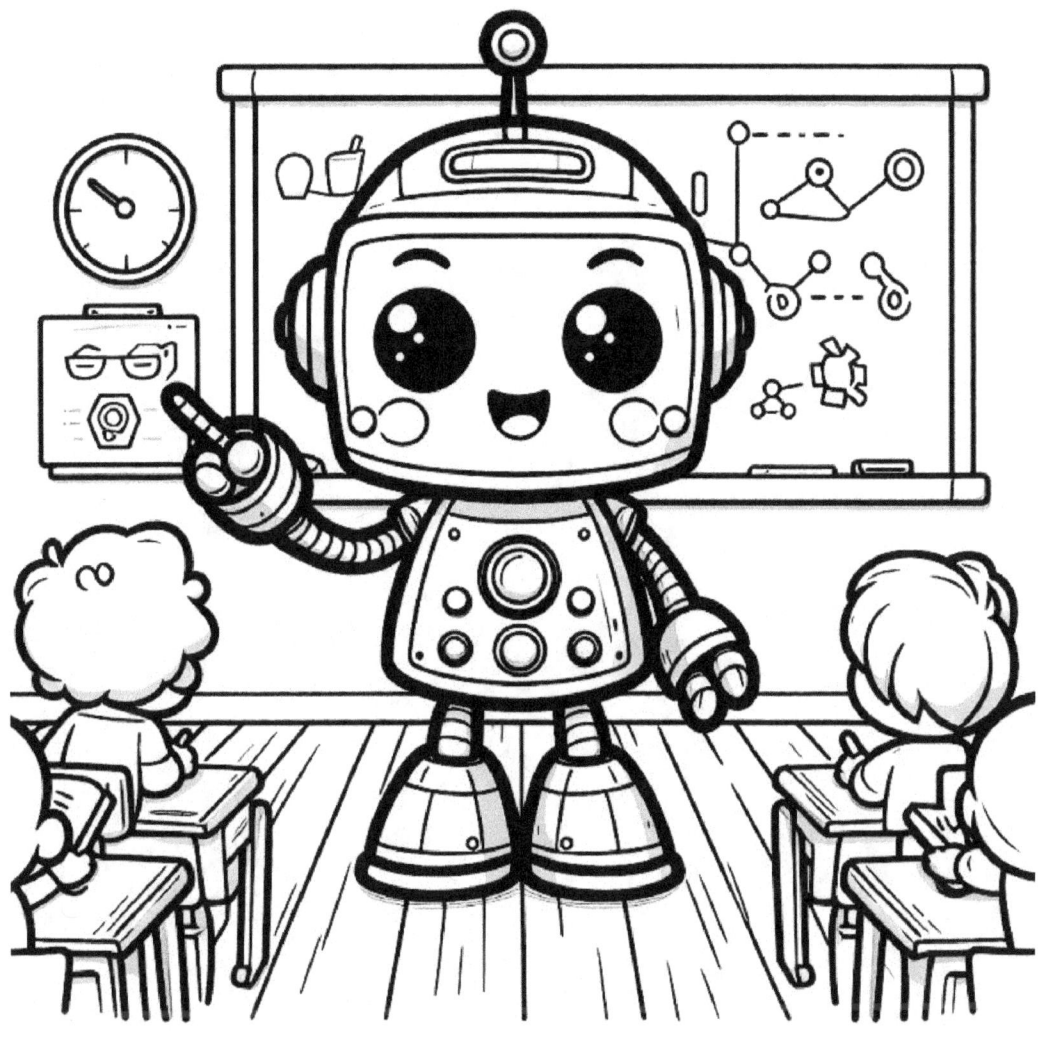

When his teacher was absent, he gave a lesson on automobiles to his classmates.

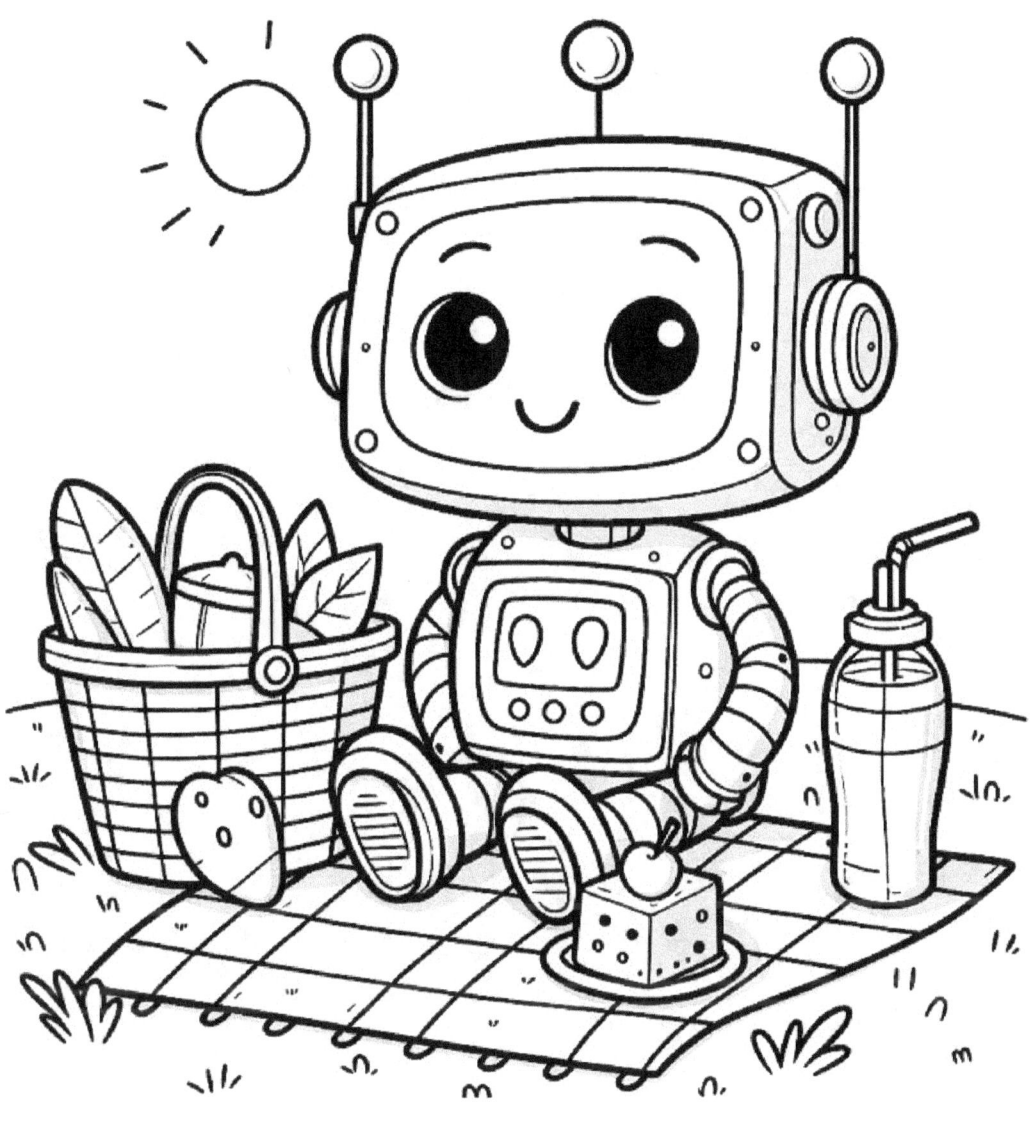

Whenever he had free time, he enjoyed having picnics in the city park.

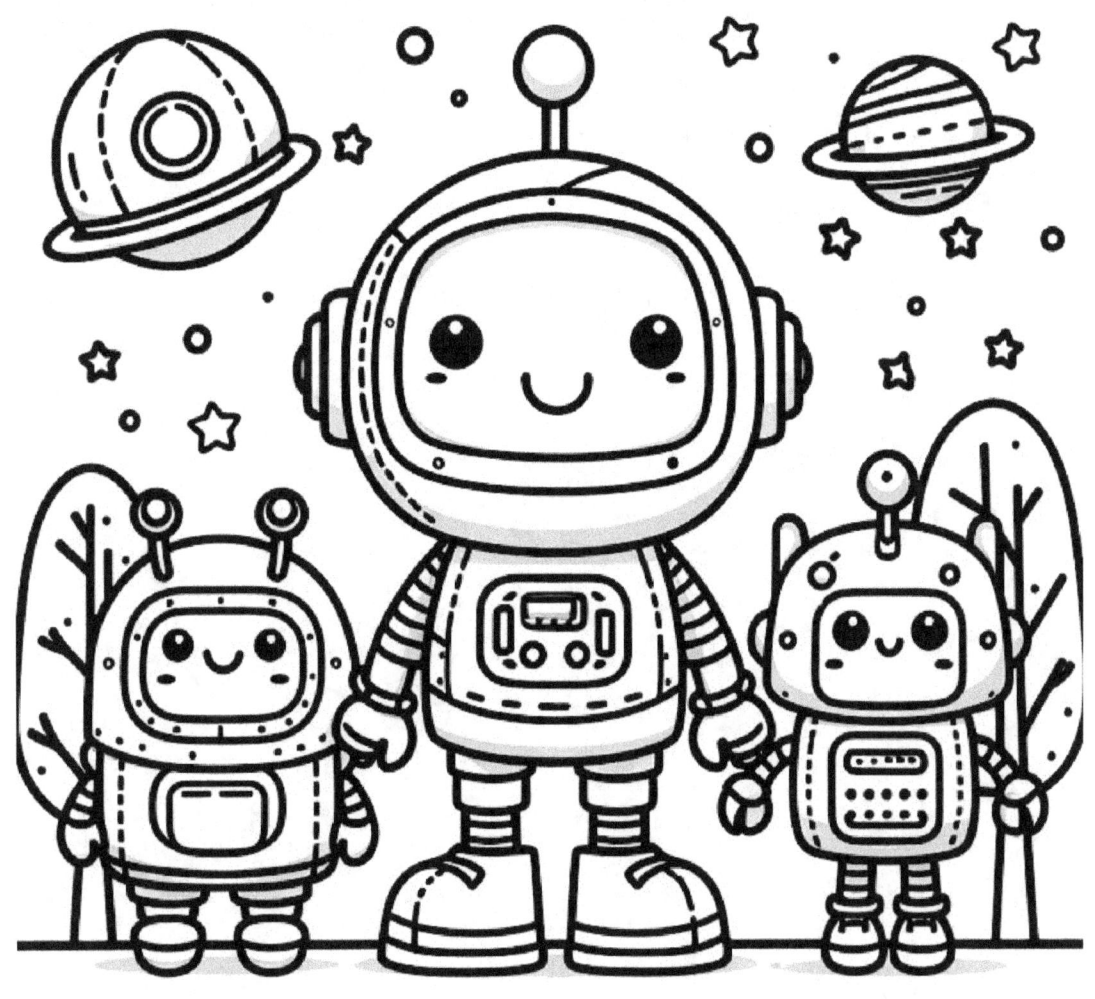

His dream was to travel to the moon with his friends.

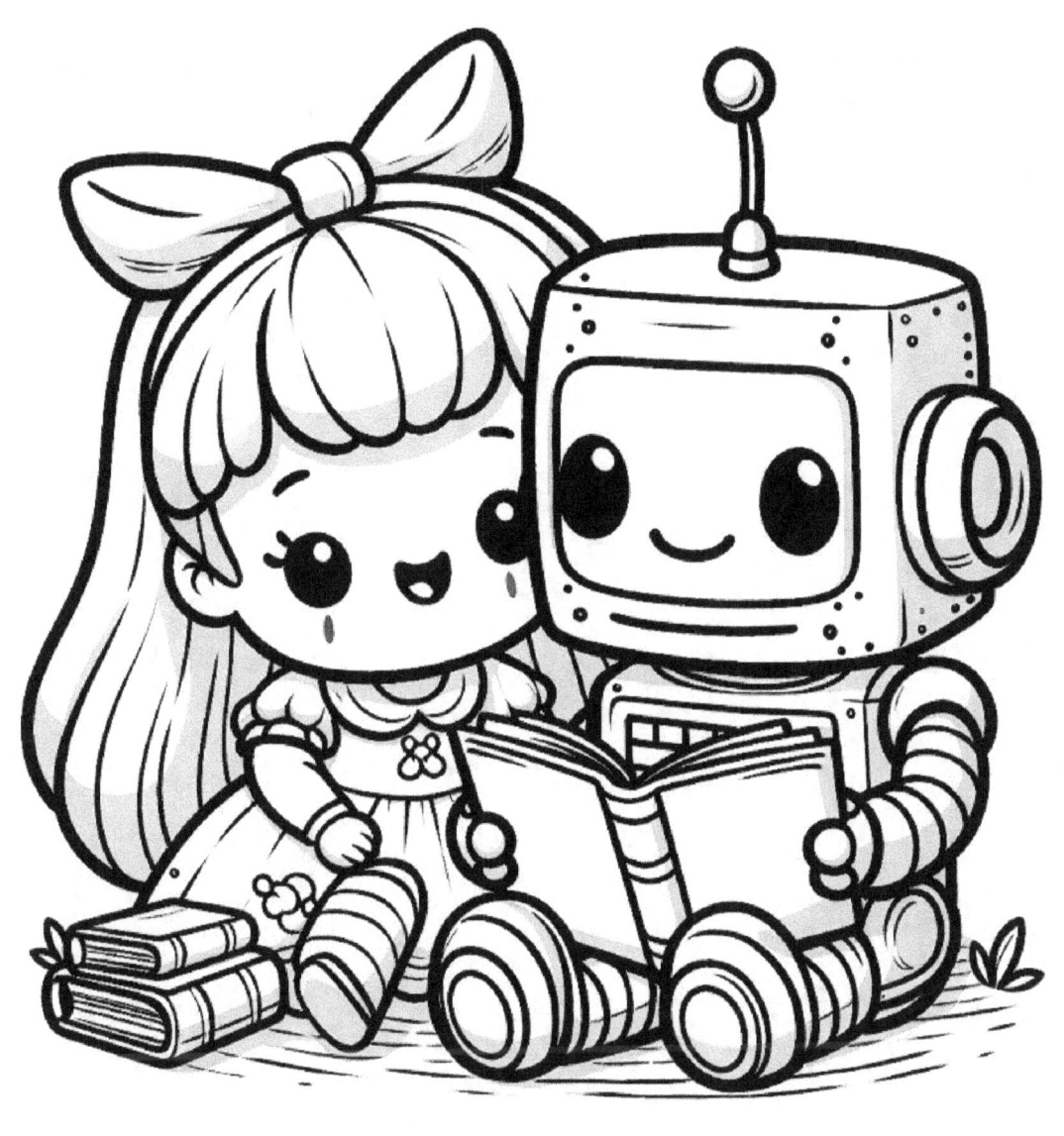

Every Sunday, he received a visit from his friend Mia.

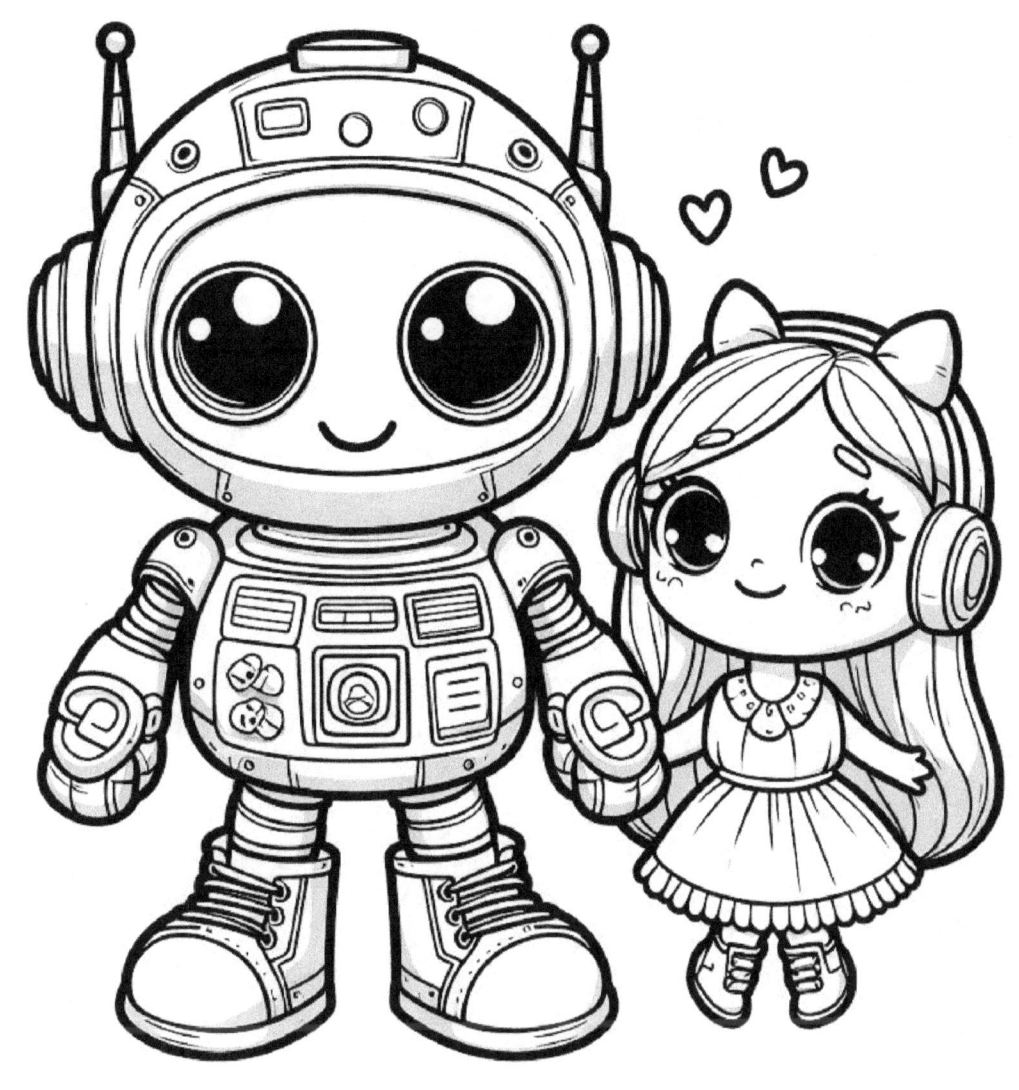

His friend Mia was a 4-year-old girl who lived in a distant neighborhood.

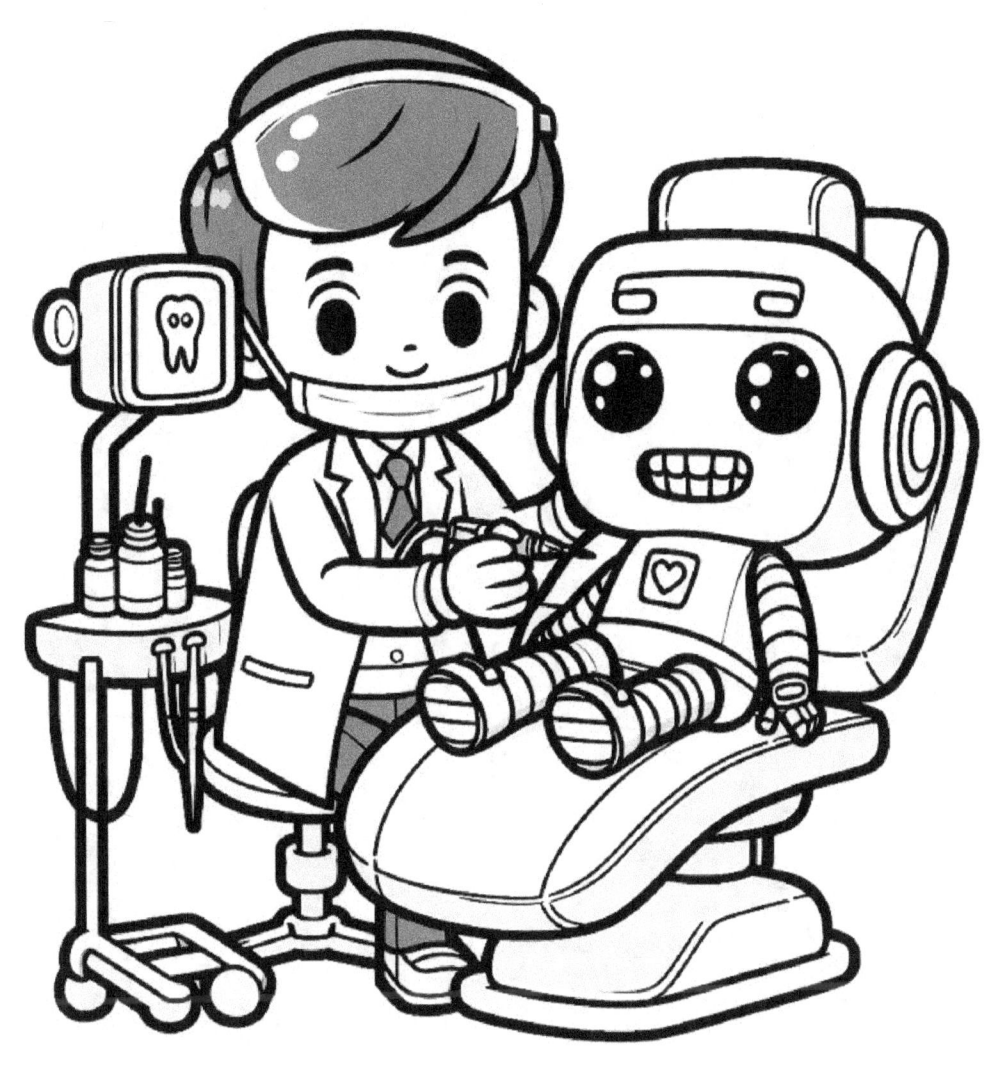

Once a year, I visited the dentist Júlio. After all, he needed to take good care of his teeth.

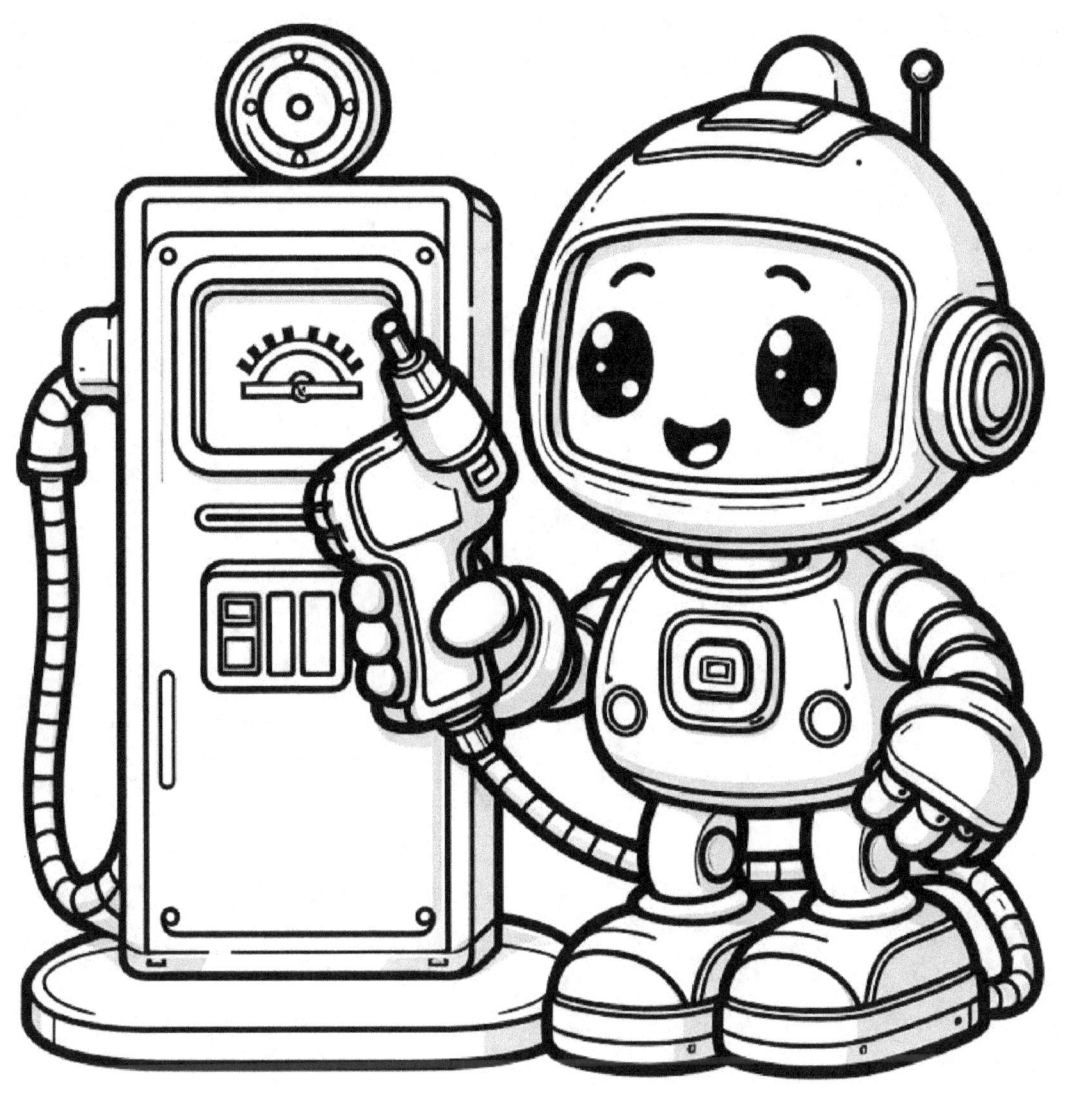

One time, when he was going to the supermaket, his car ran out of gas, and Nitti Liky had to refuel.

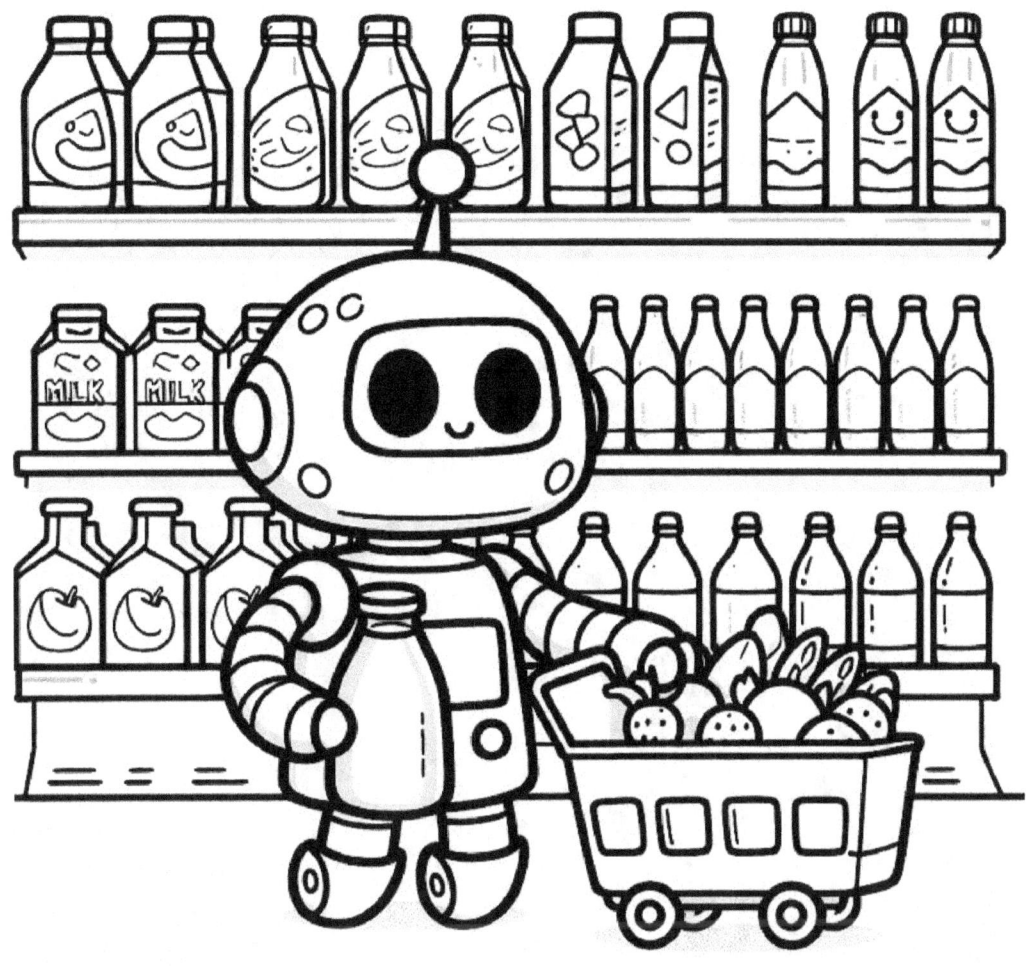

At the supermarket, the floor was wet, and he didn't see it, so he slipped.

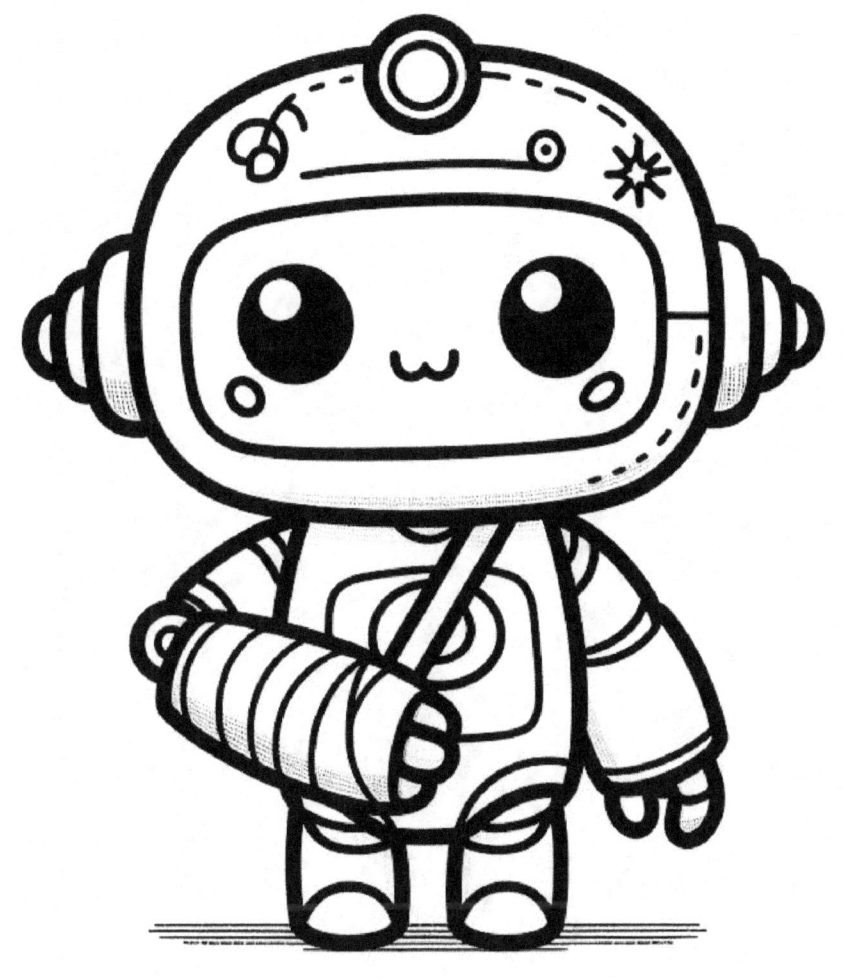

He had his arm in a cast for a month.

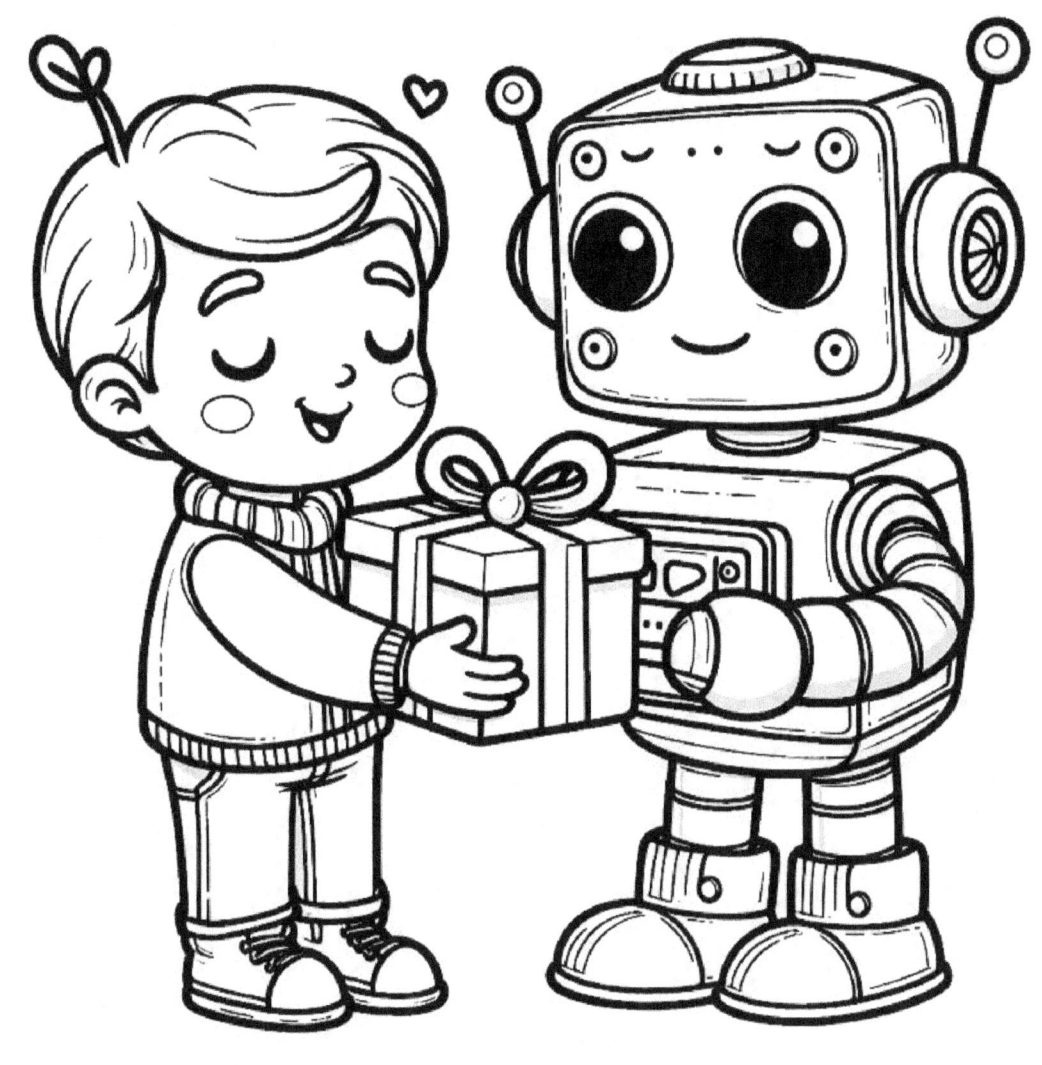

On his birthday, his friend Peter gave him a beautiful box as a present.

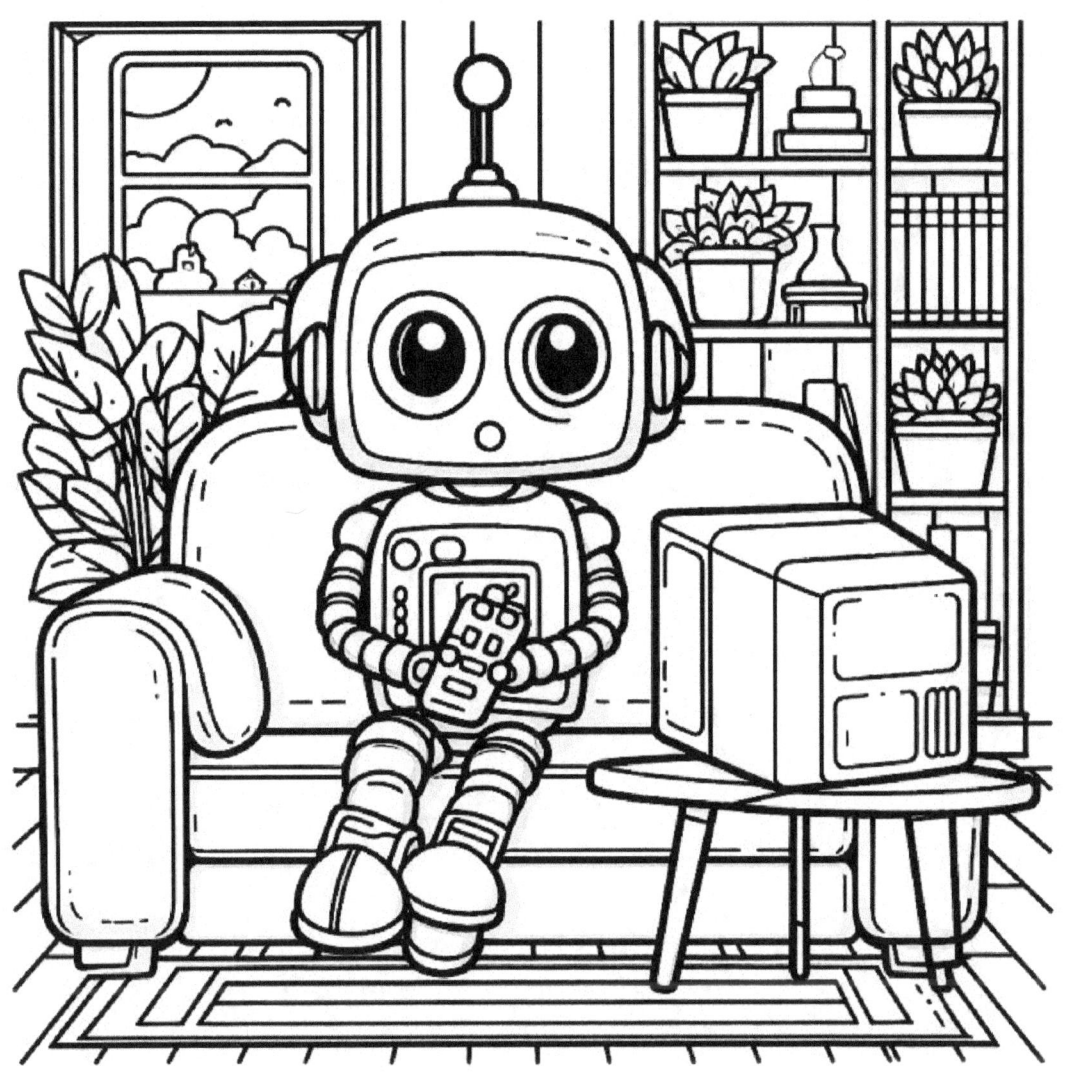

At night, he watched the news on TV.

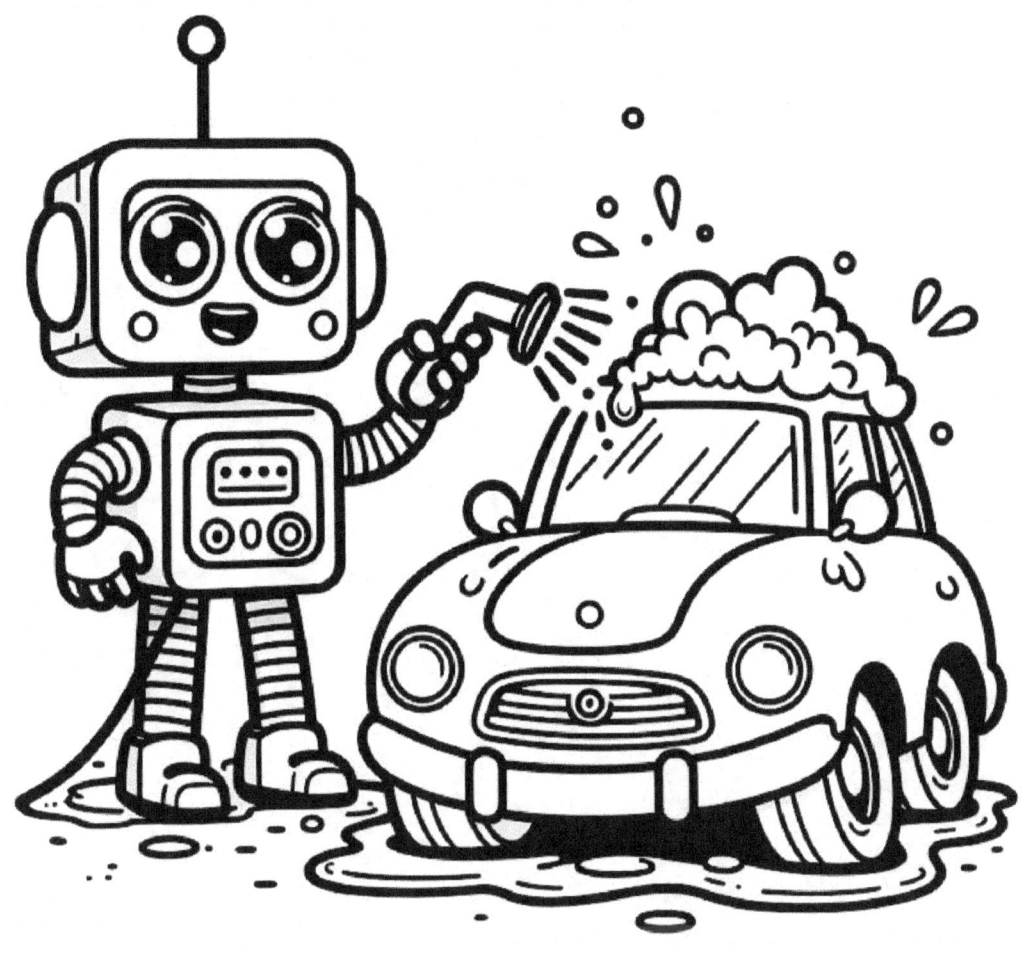

On weekends, he washed his car..

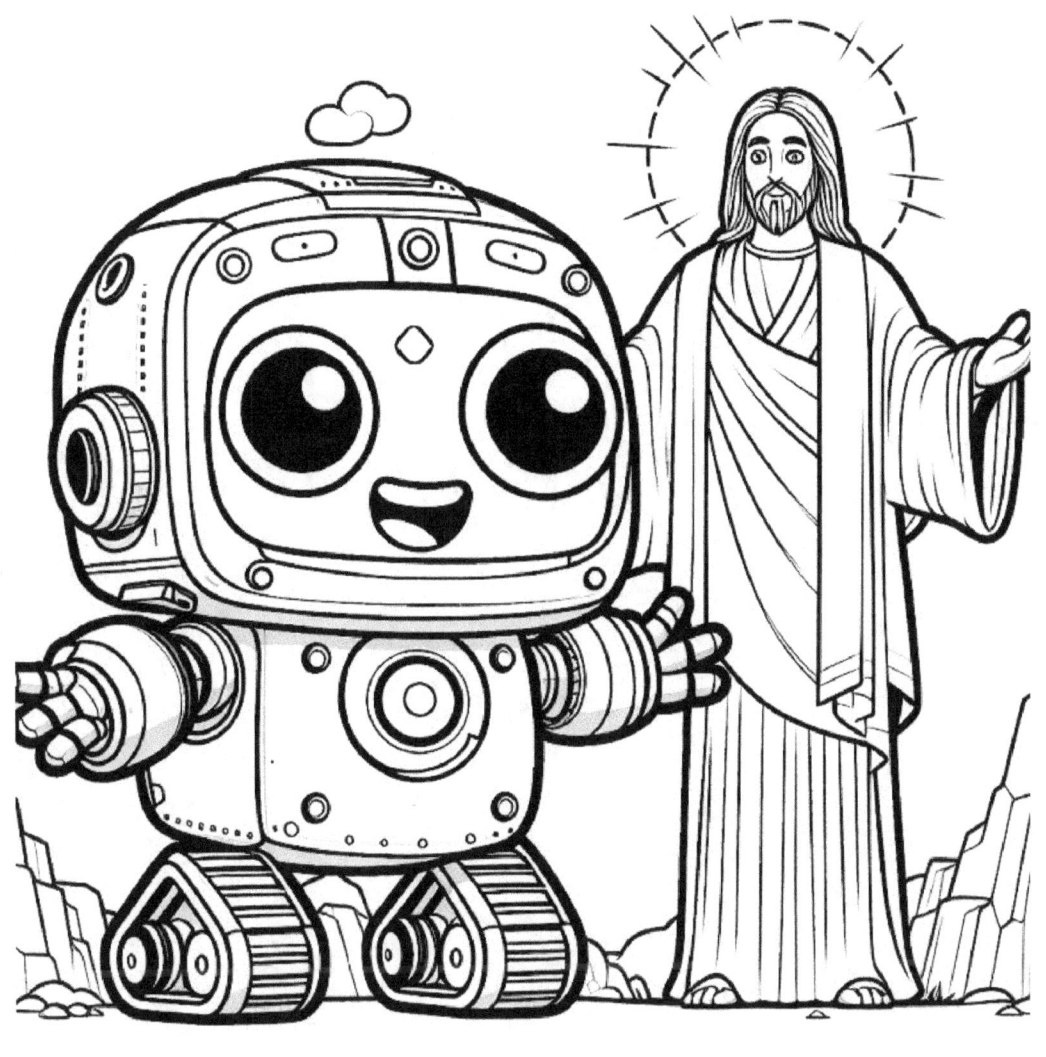

He liked to see the statue of Christ the Redeemer in the city.

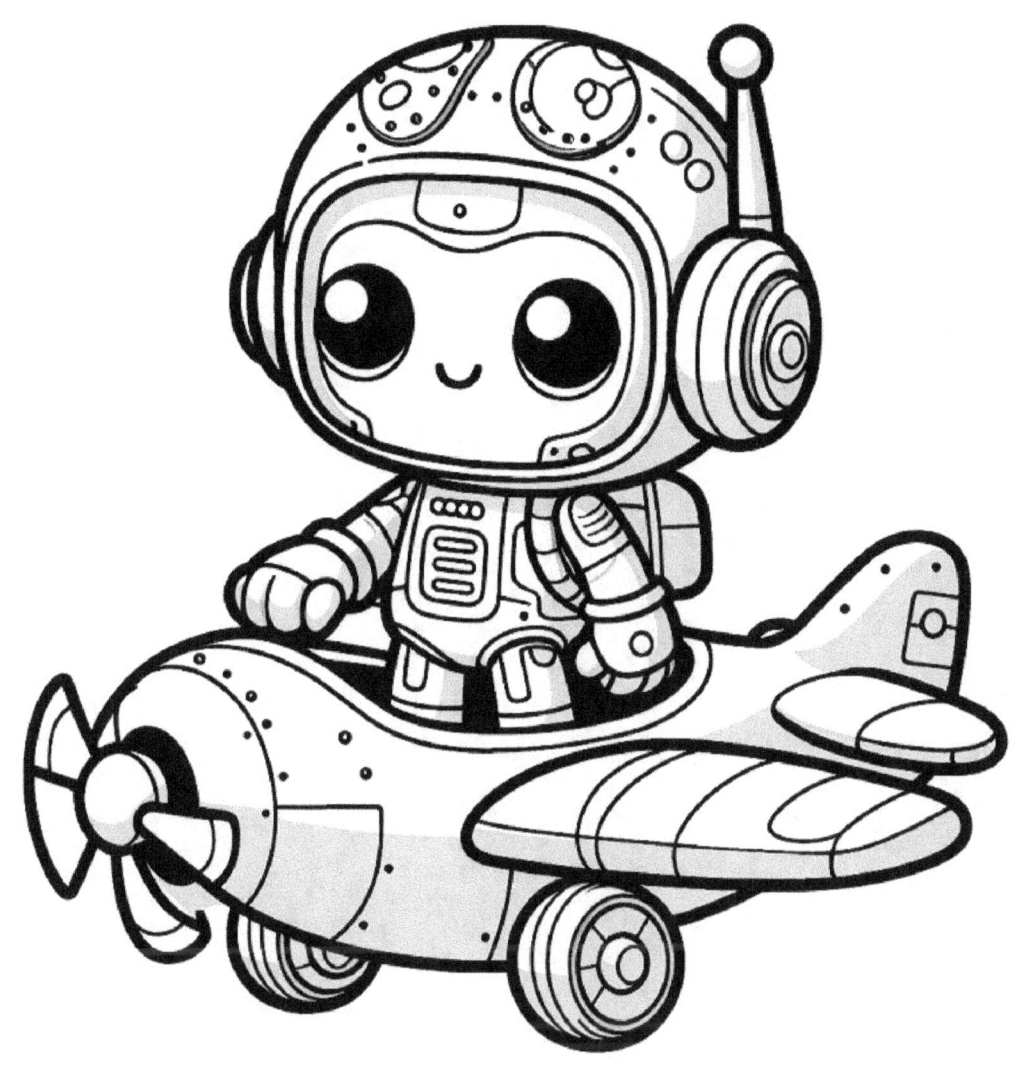

In the autumn, he piloted his plane to visit his friends.

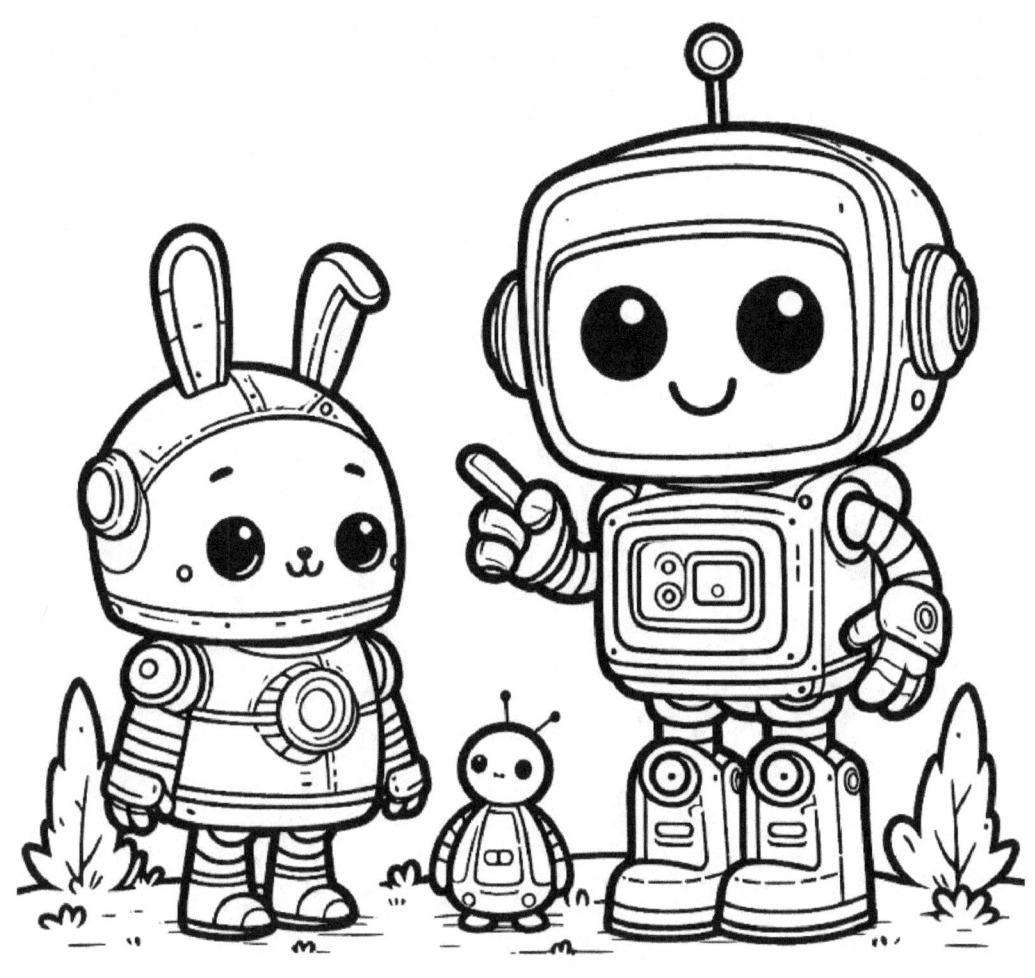

During autumn, he visited his friends Gael and Rael in the neighboring city.

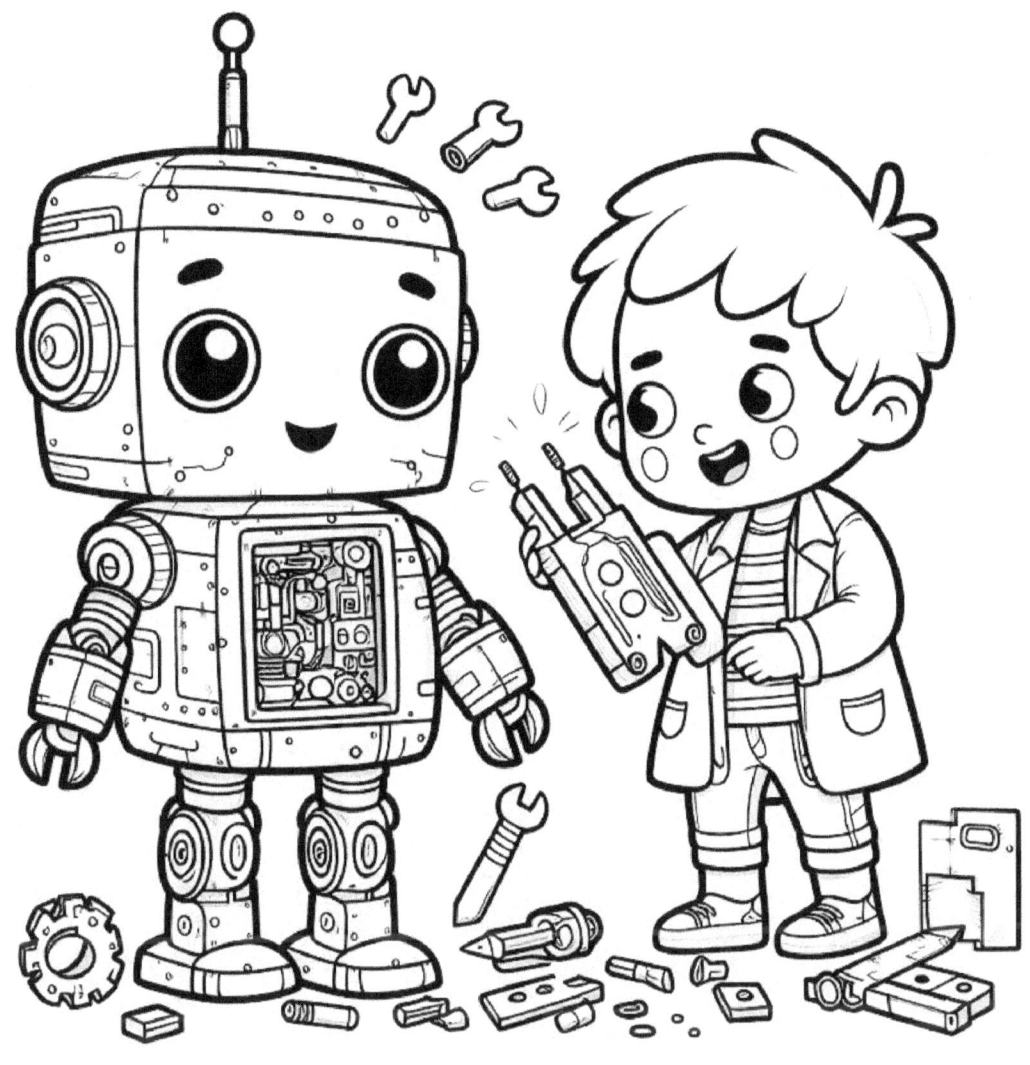

One day, he didn't wake up feeling well and went to the doctor to see what the problem was.

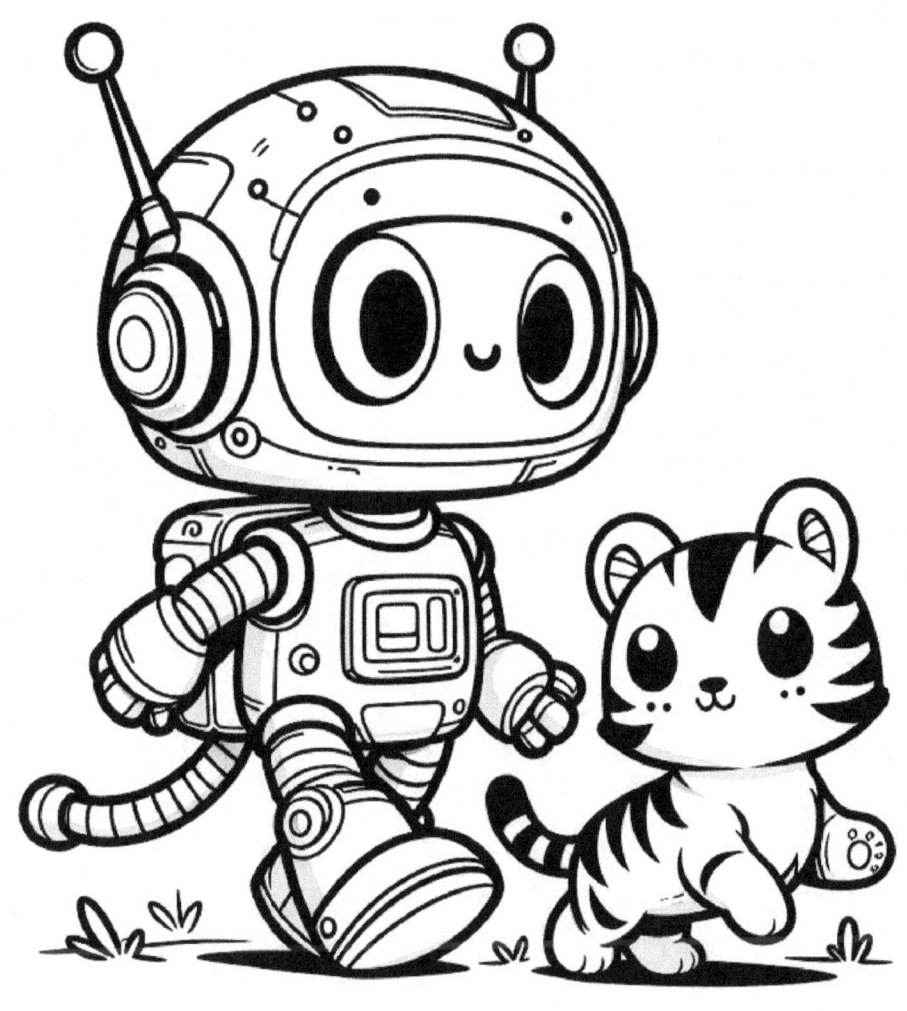

Little Tiger was one of Niti Liky's favorite animals

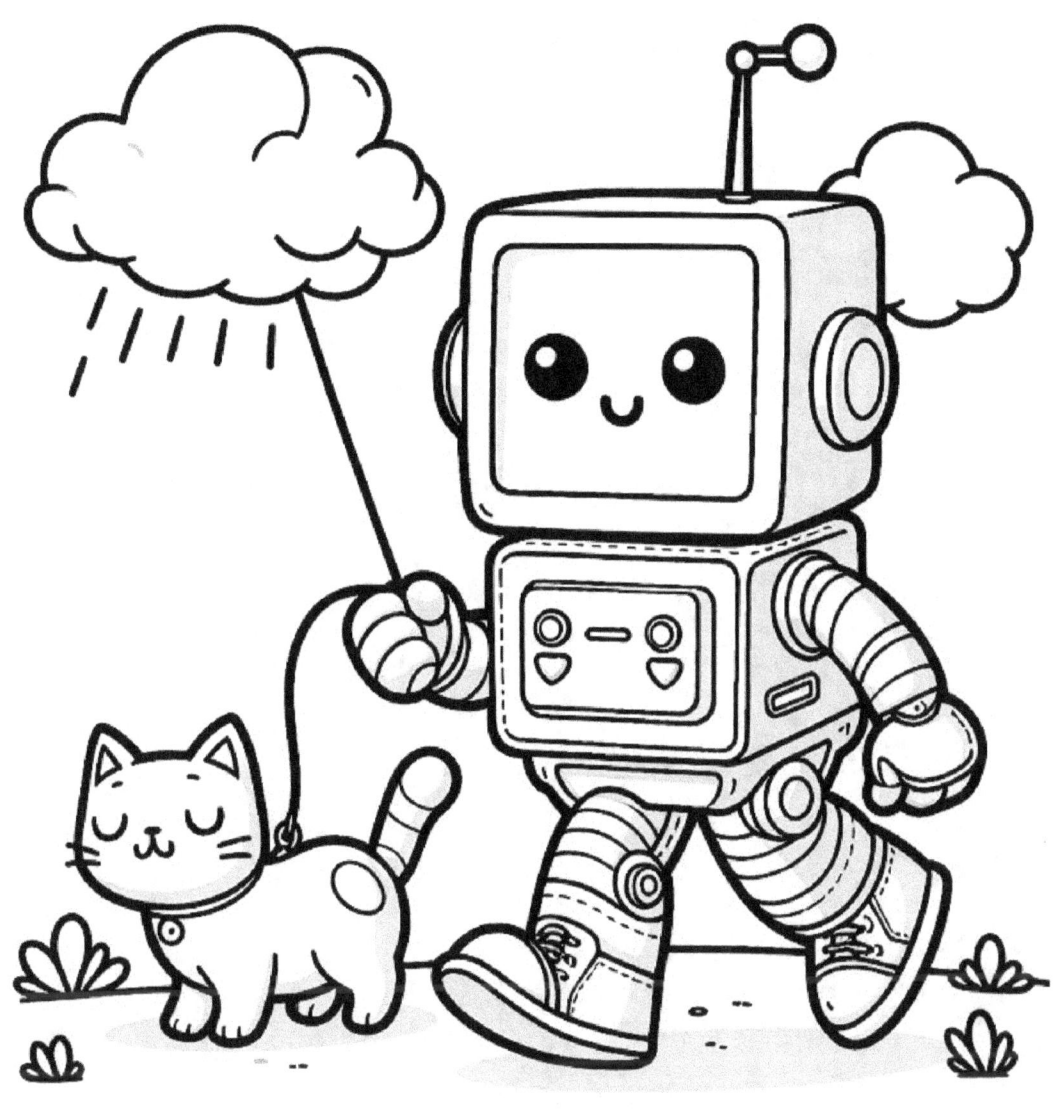

But he had the kitten Ted who always accompanied him on walks.

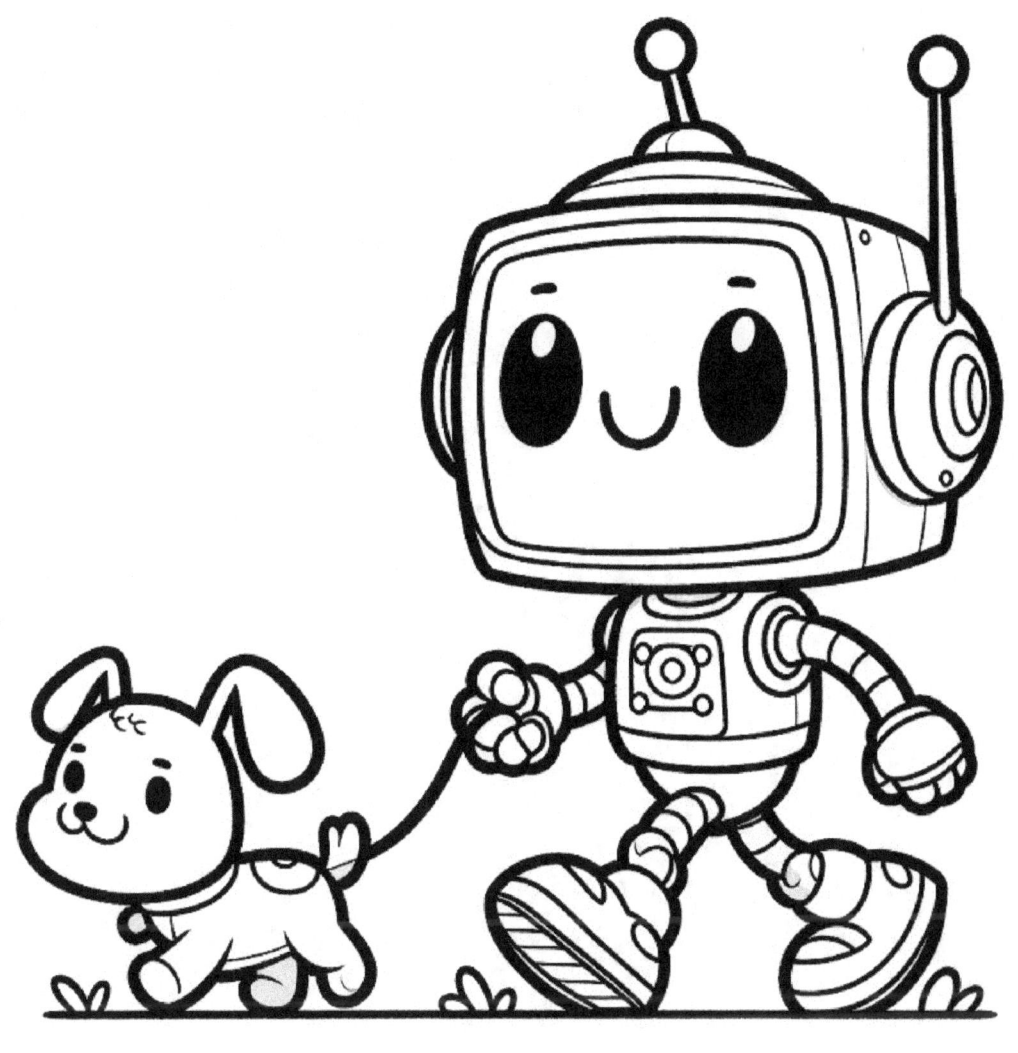

When Ted wasn't with him, he took his little dog Max with him.

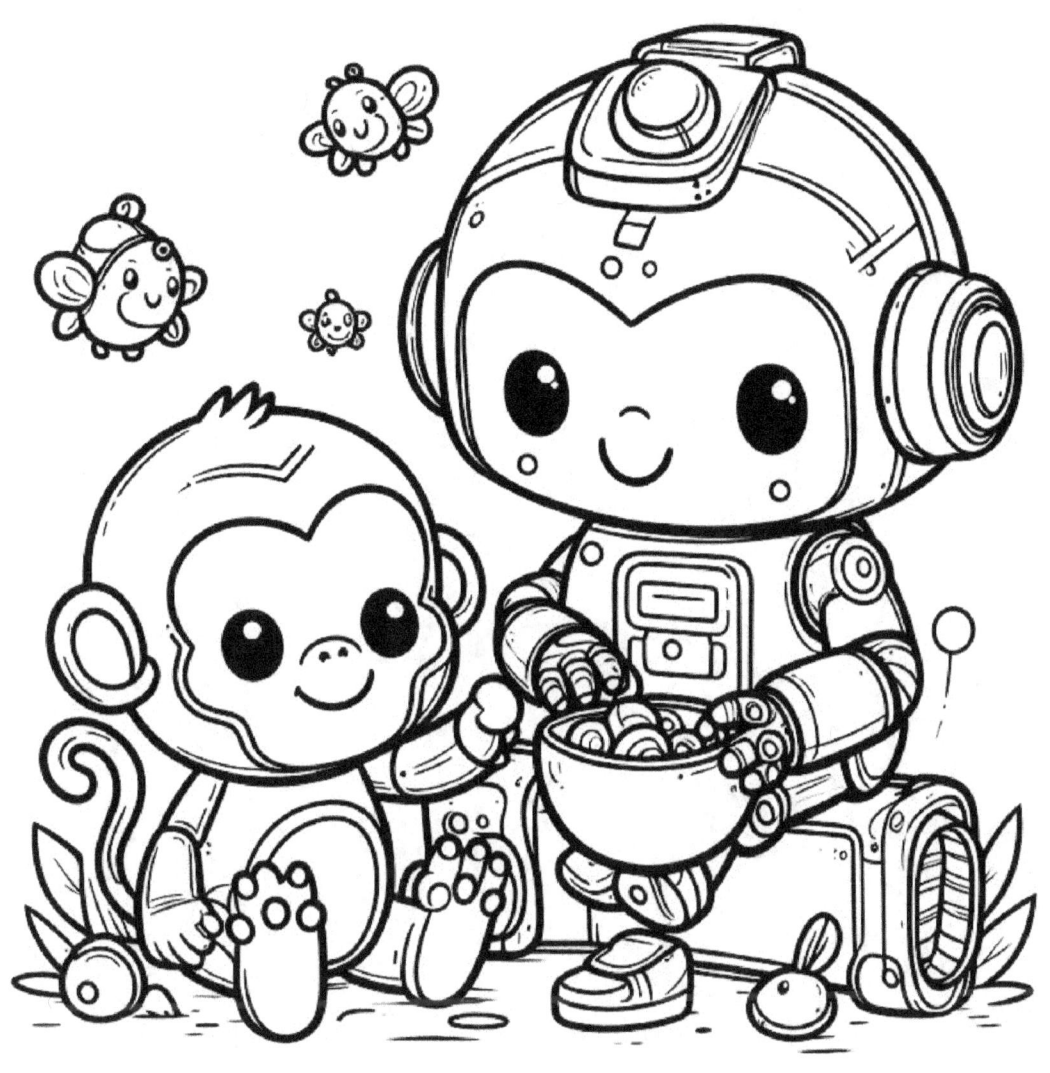

Niti Lily never forgot to feed the little monkey Bob, who always ran away to the neighbor's yard.

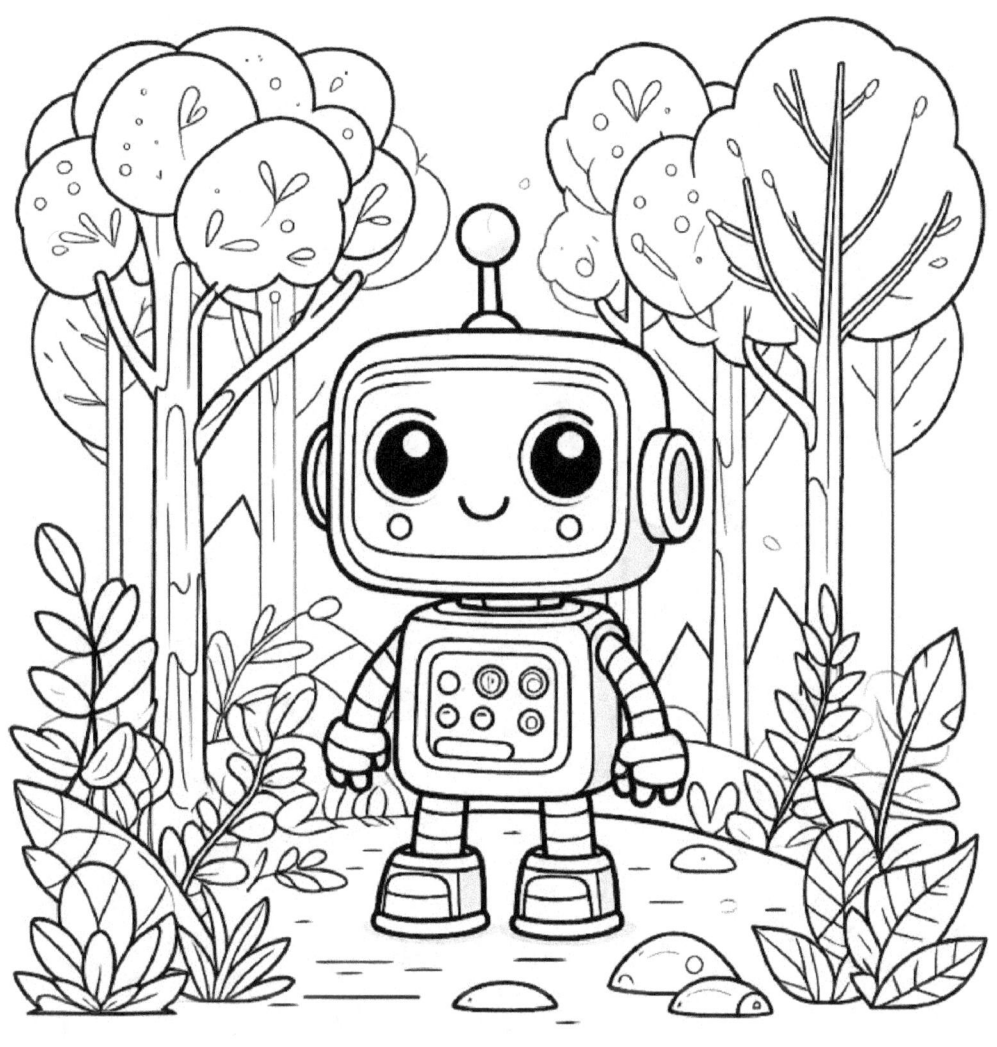

Niti Liky always searched for his little monkey around the neighborhood.

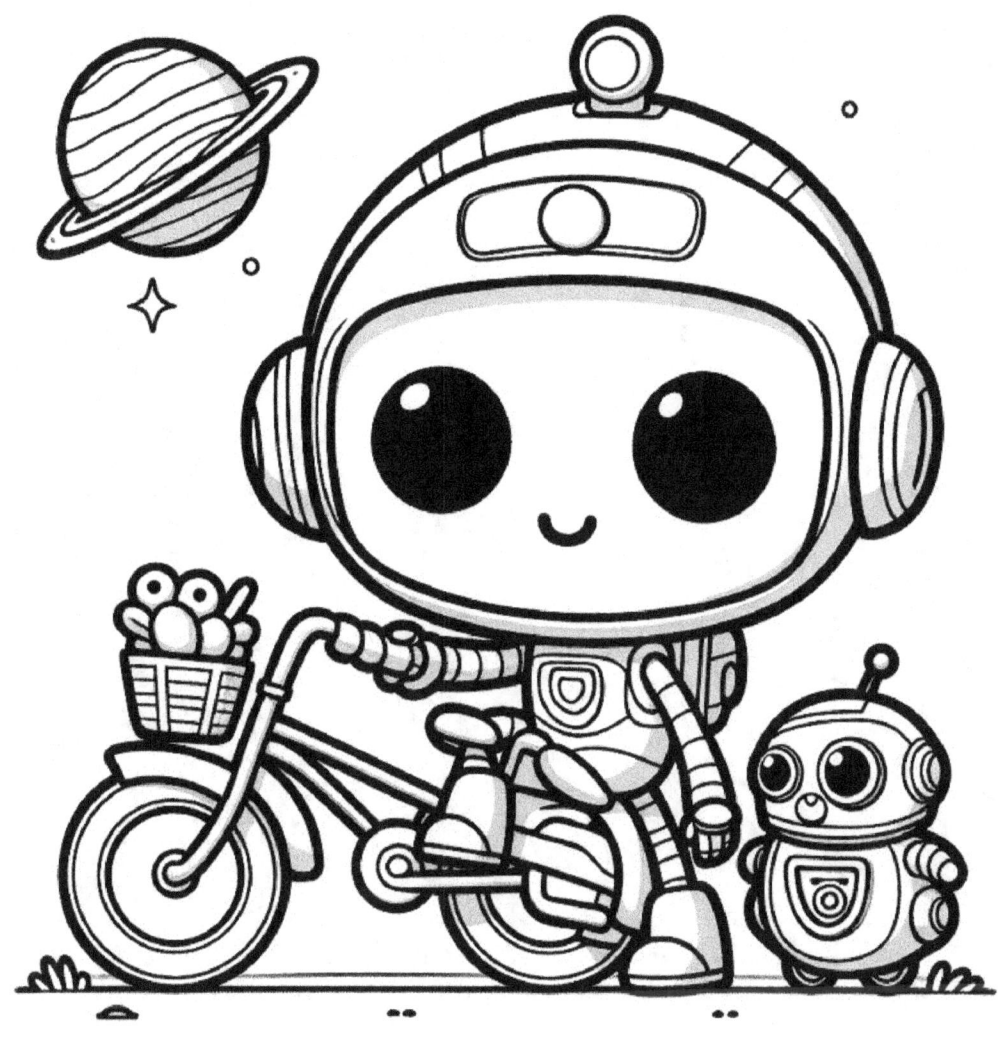

Sometimes he would ride his bicycle around the neighborhood.

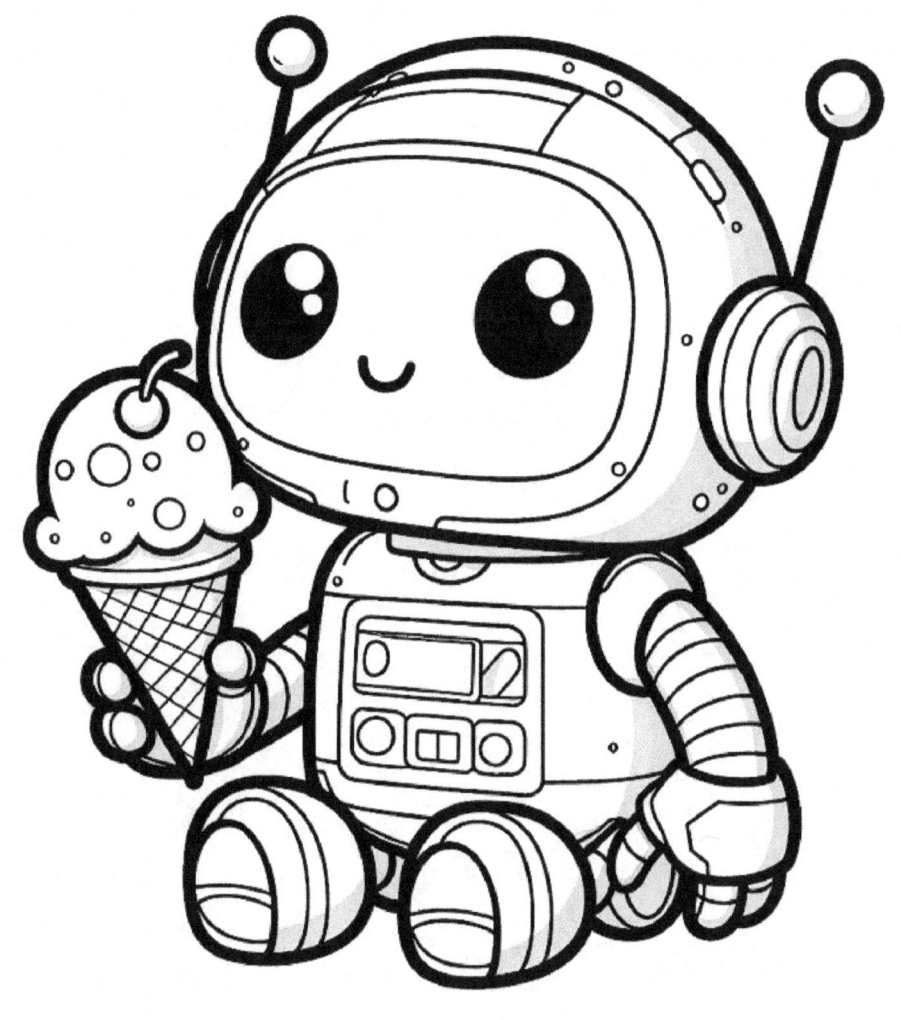

On very hot days, he would have an ice cream in the city center.

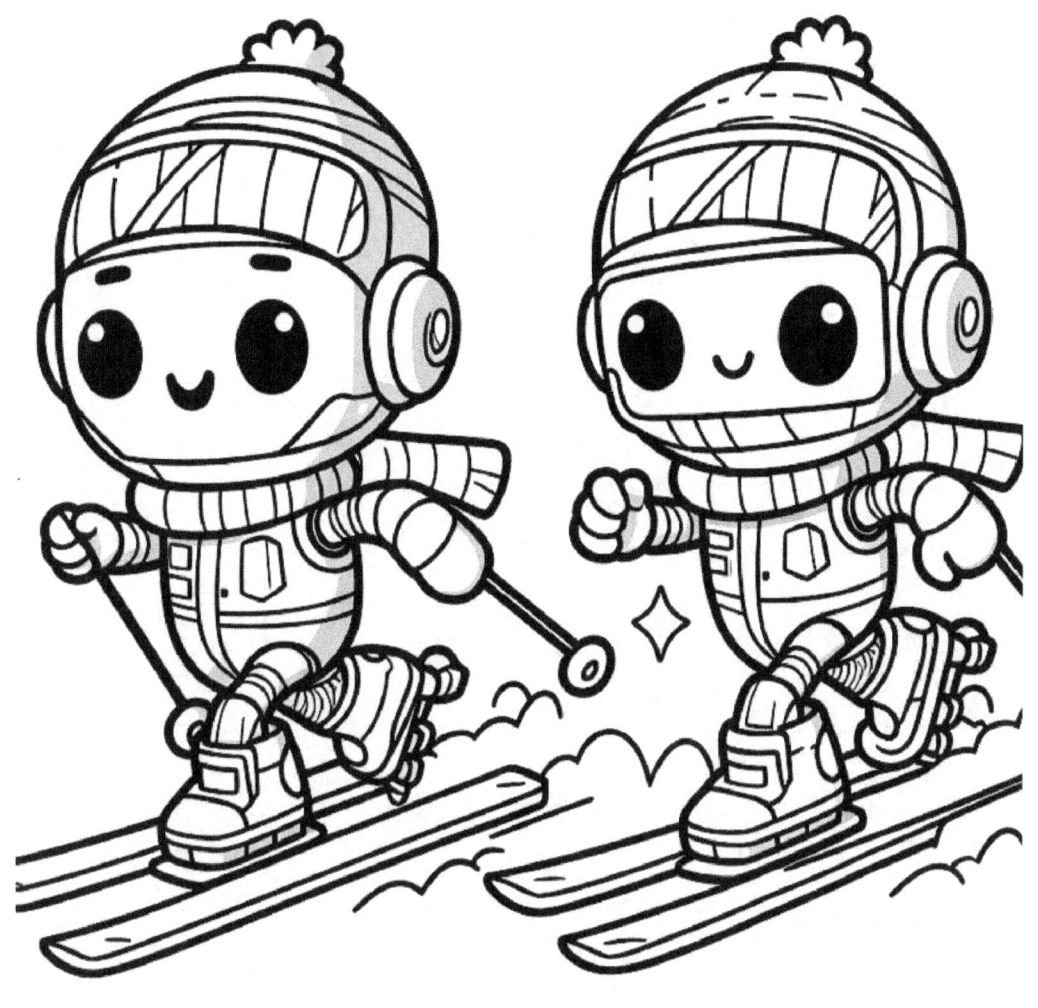

During school holidays, he went skiing in the mountains with his friend Peter.

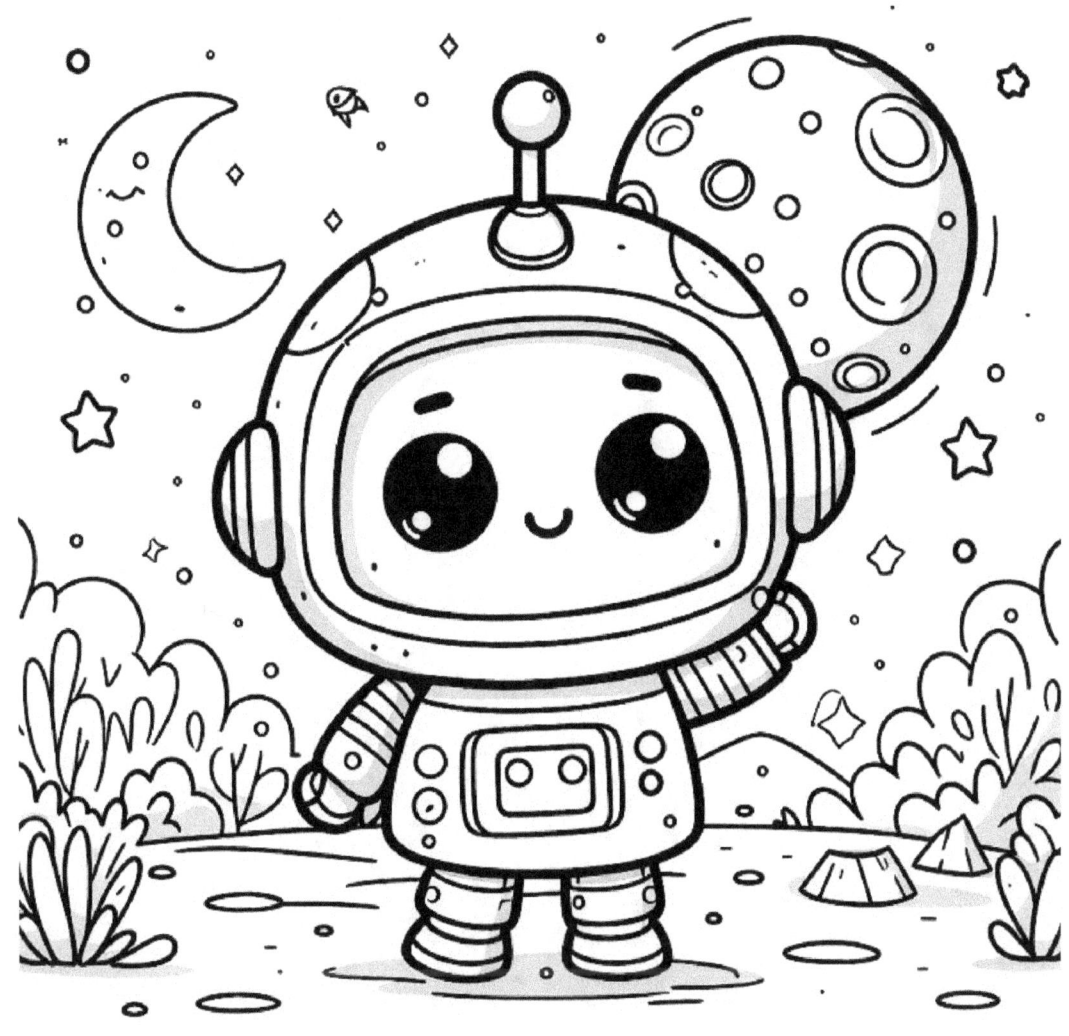

He never left home without informing his parents so they wouldn't worry.

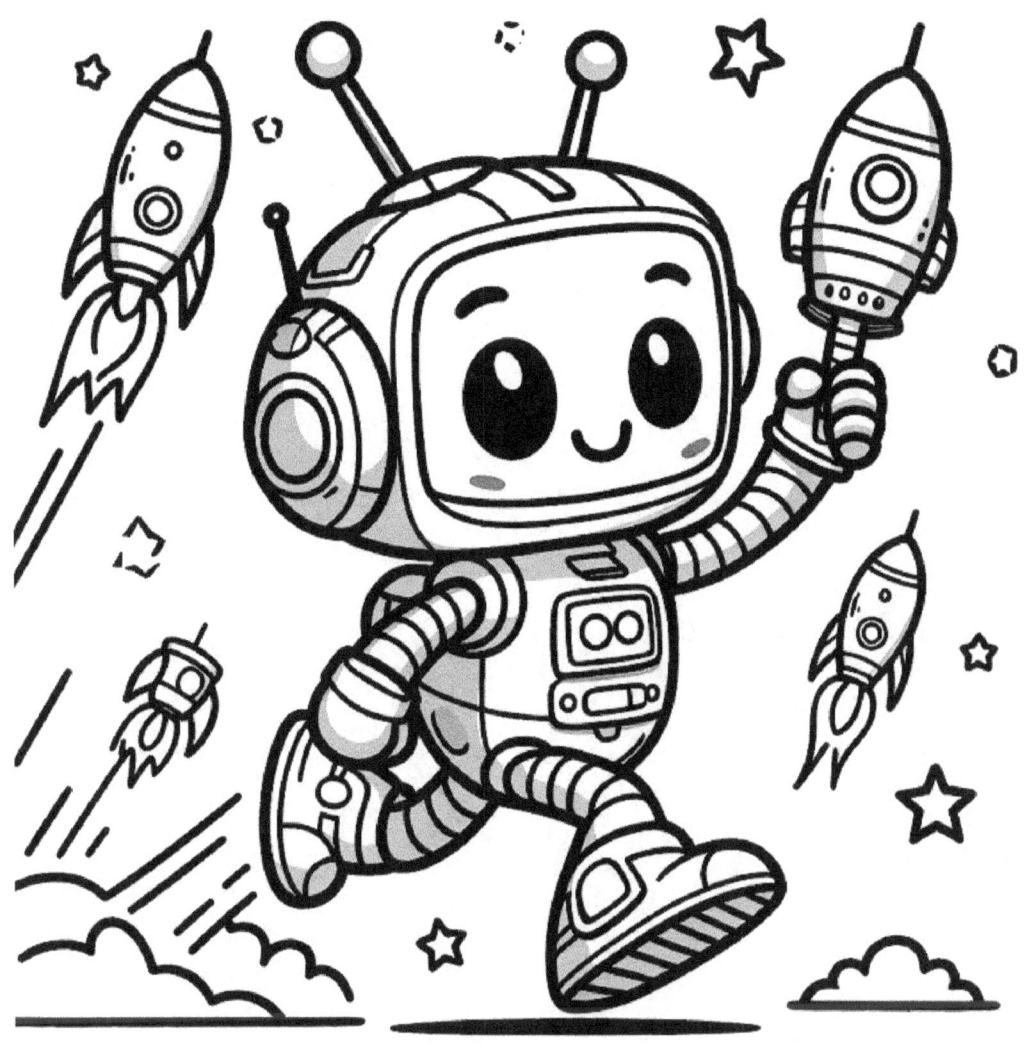

At the science fair, Niti Liky created a rocket that split into three parts, which startled everyone.

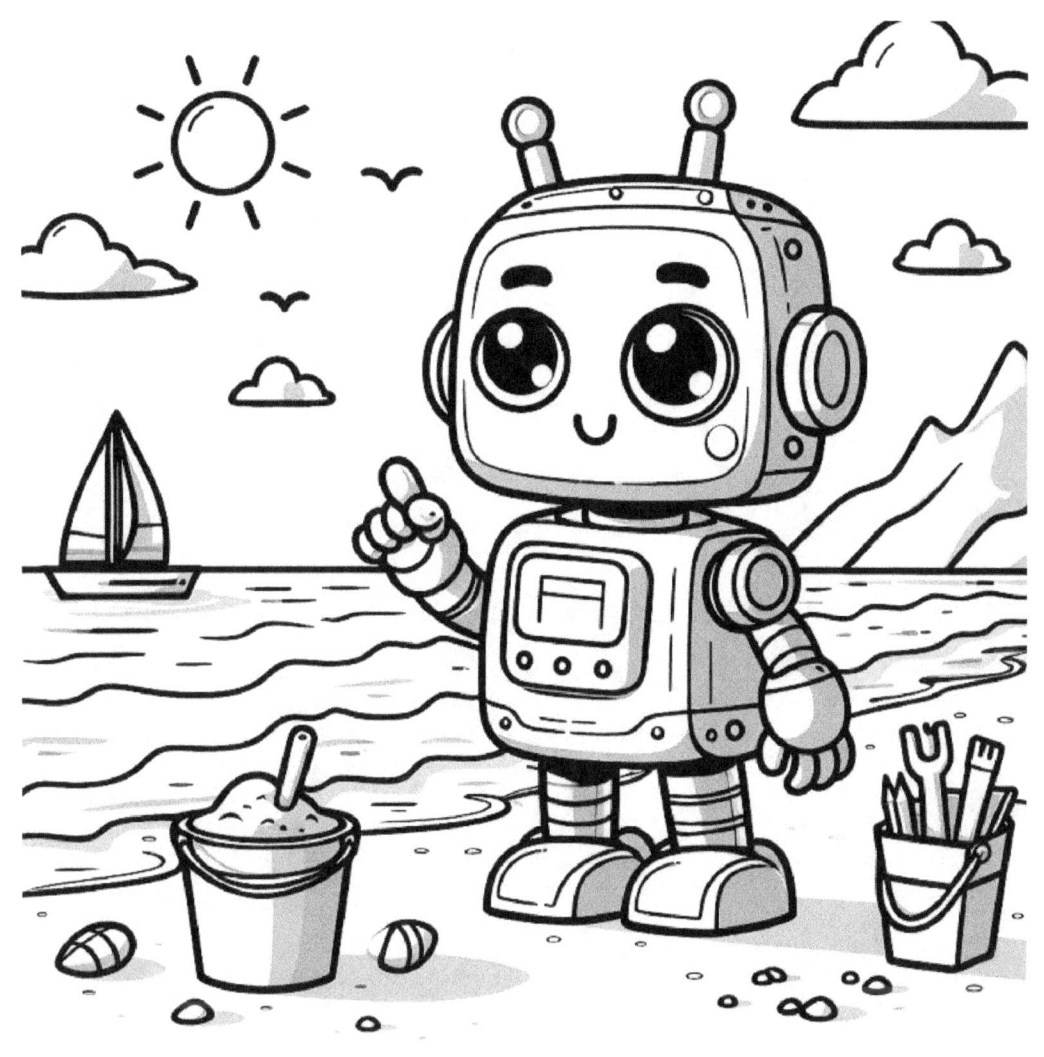

Niti Liky was brave... he wanted to prove that robots could also go to the beach... and he did... but he didn't apply sunscreen and got burnt all over.

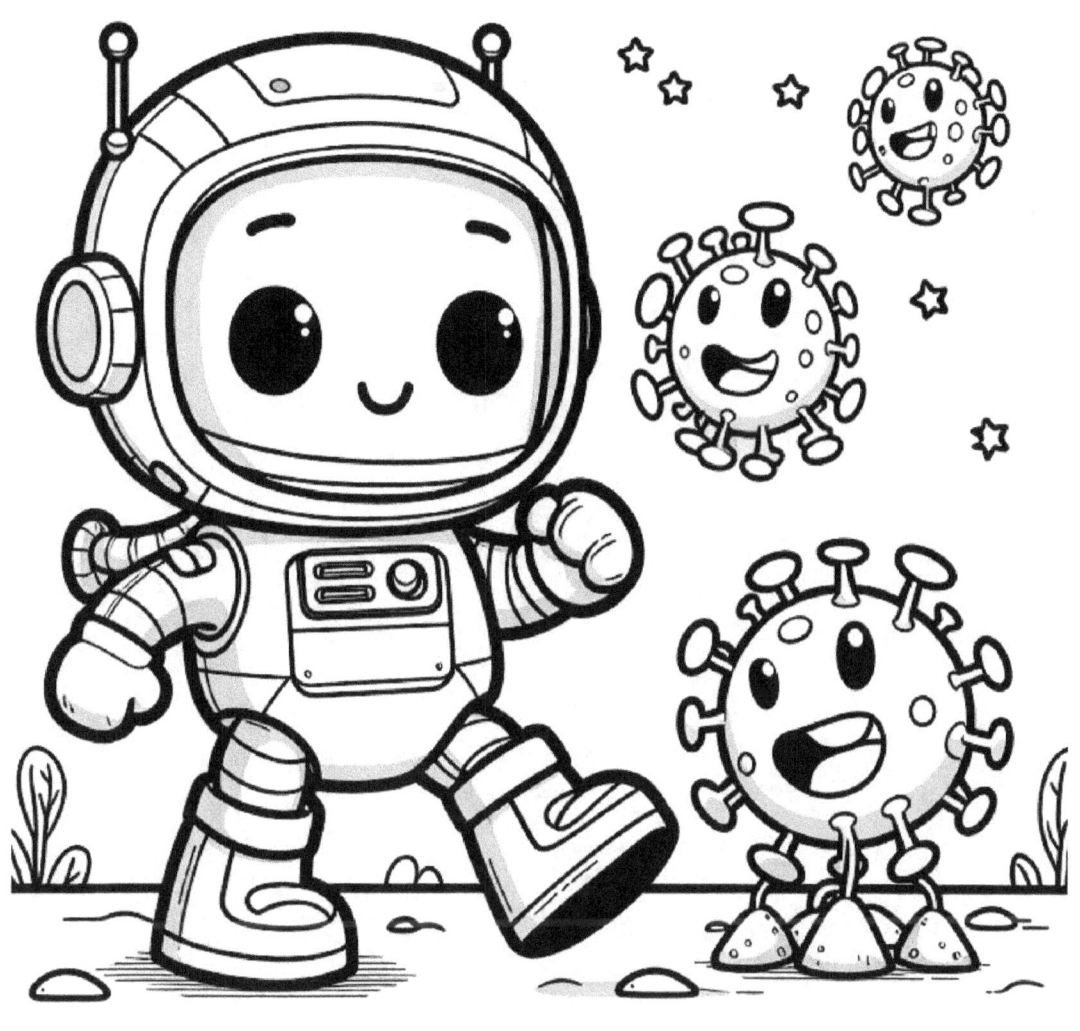

During the pandemic, he fought against viruses and defeated them all.

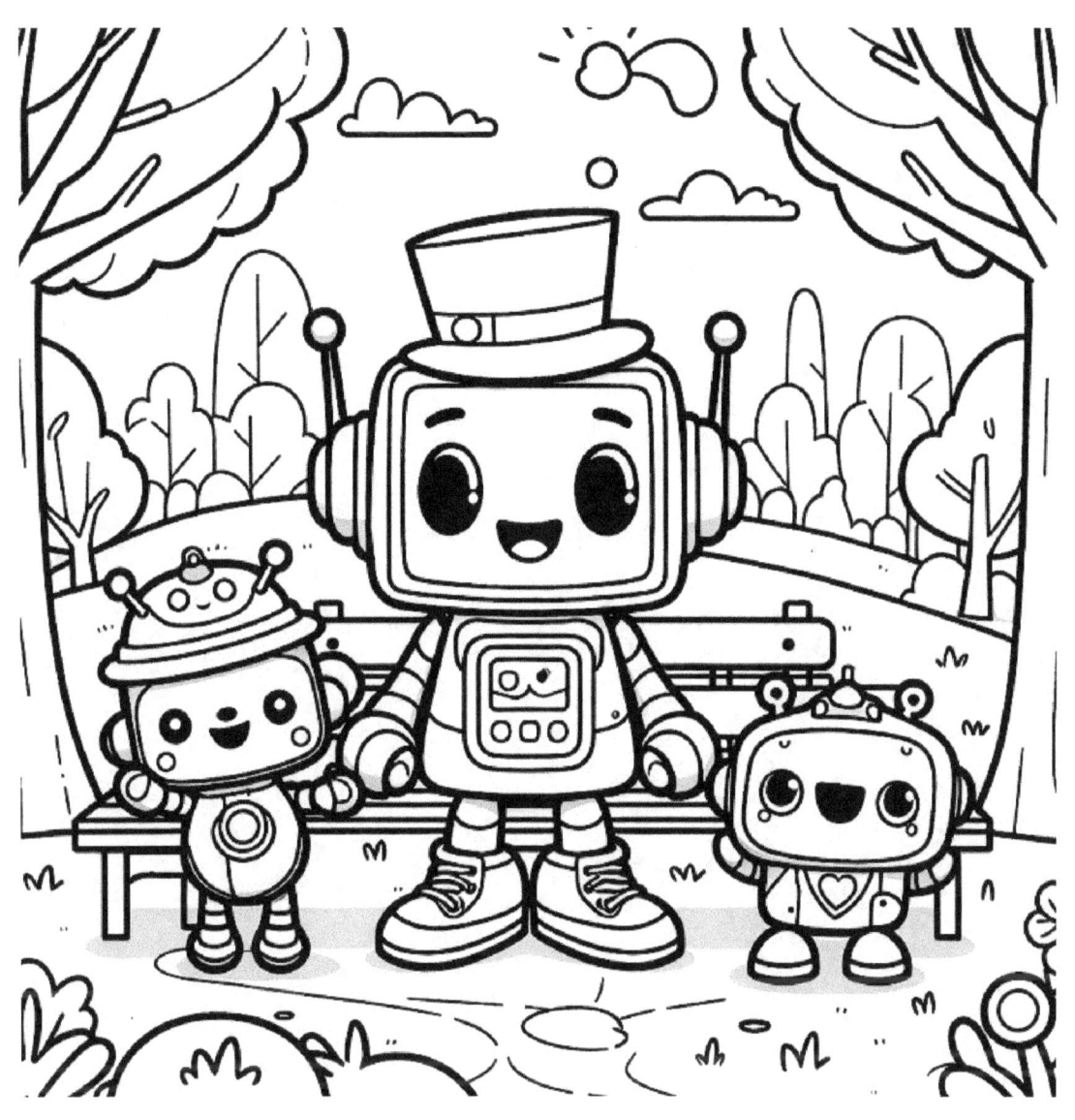

He found two cousins in the city park.

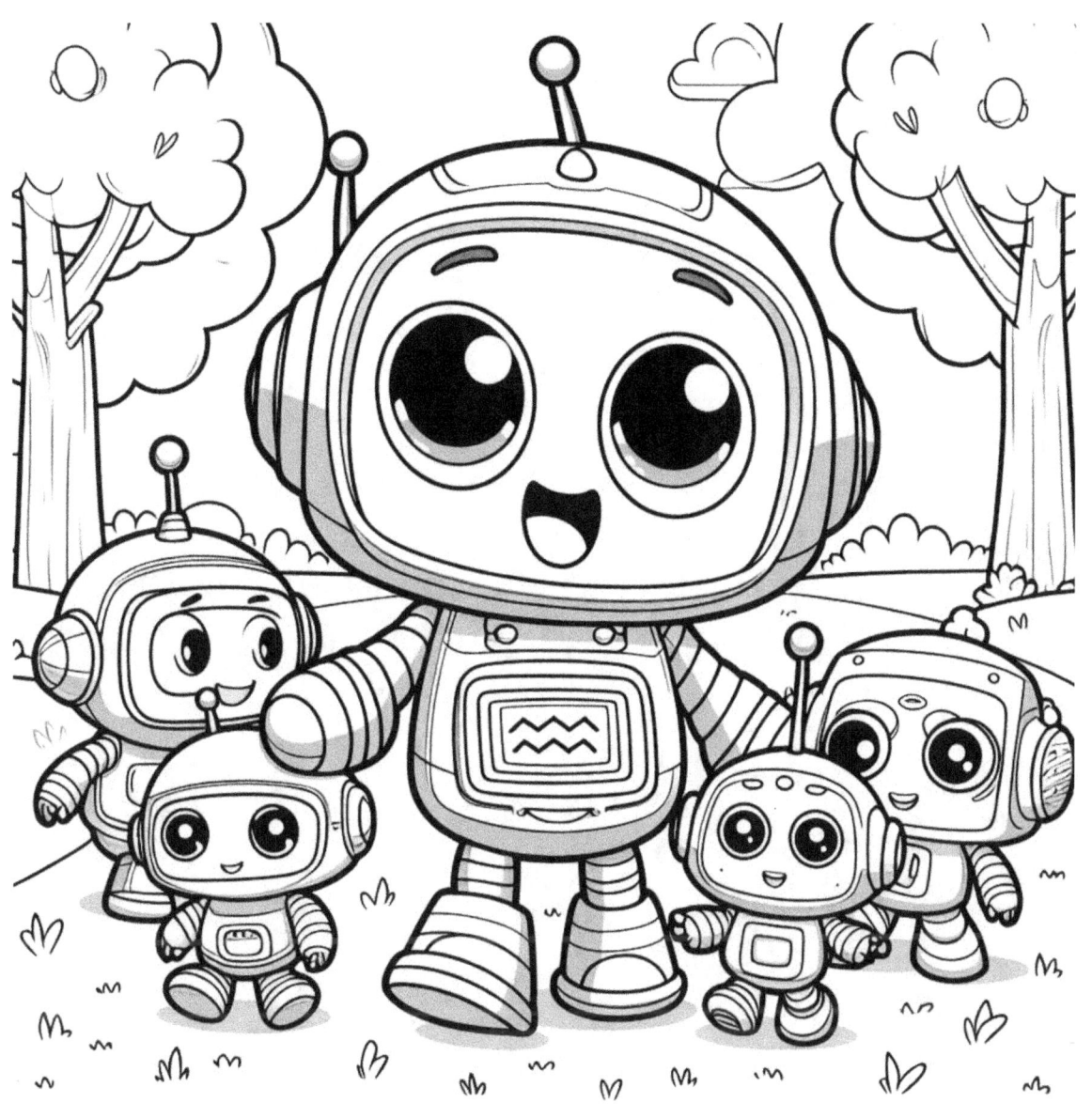

Still in the city park, he talked to his neighbors and schoolmates.

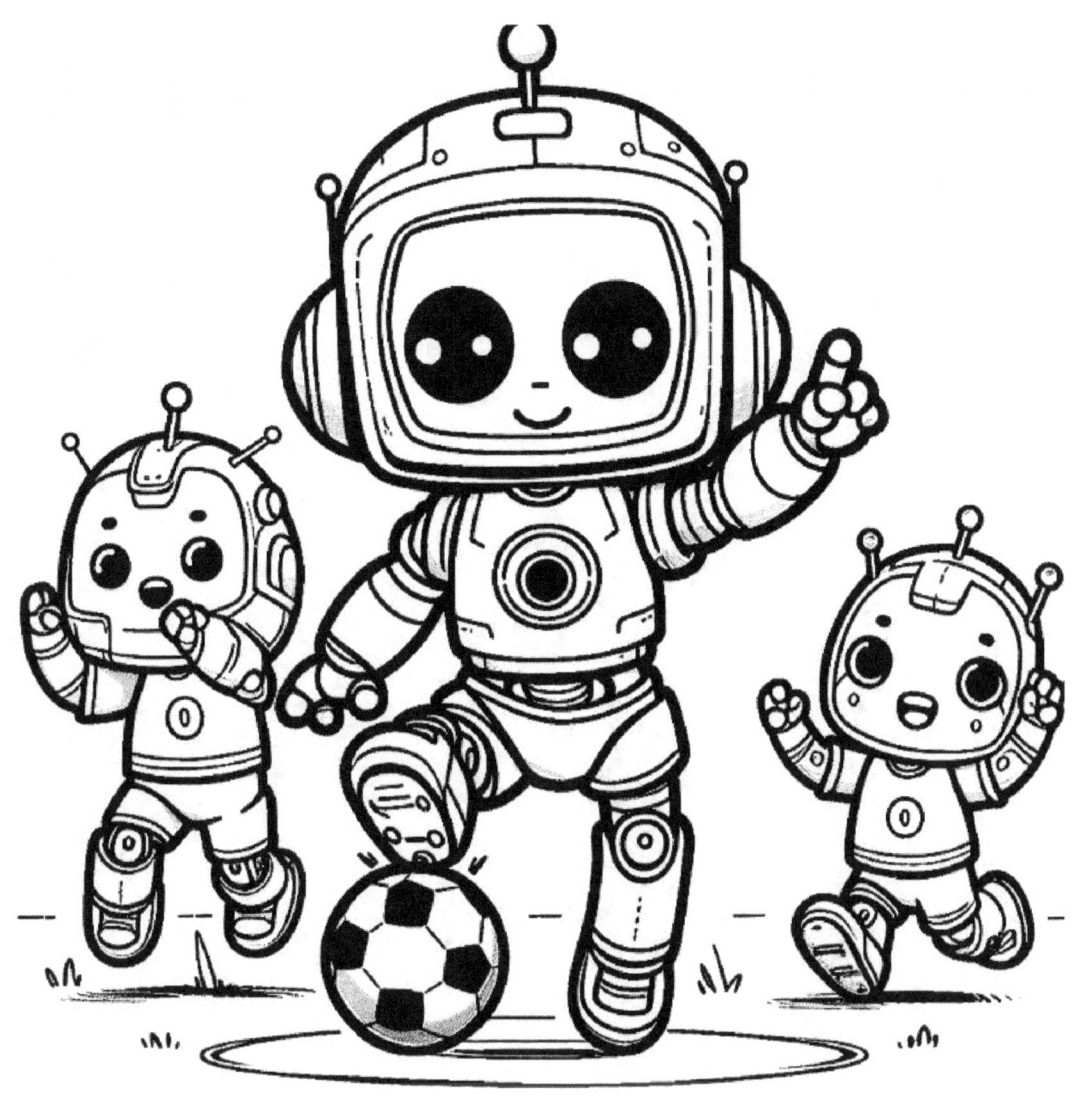

And in the end he played football with his friends...It was a fun game!

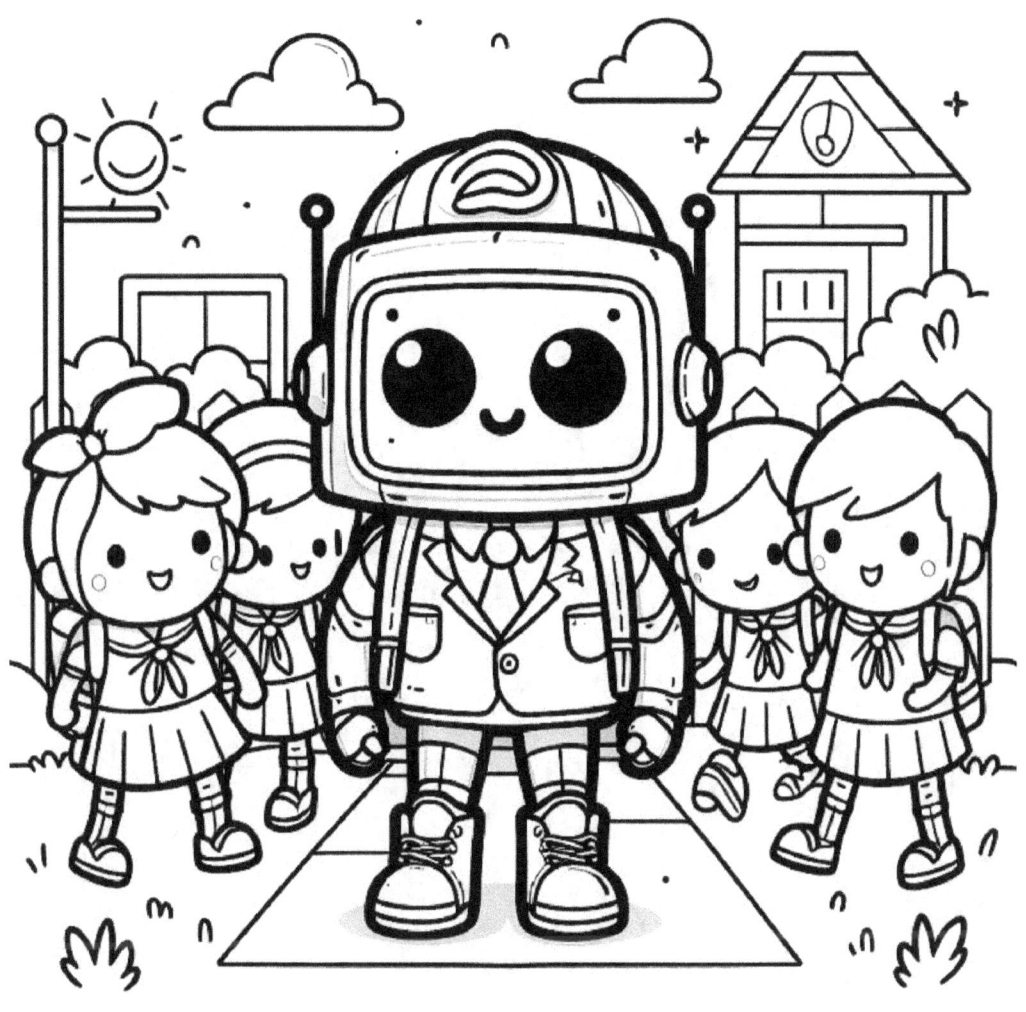

On his first day of school, his classmates were amazed to see a robot attending school.

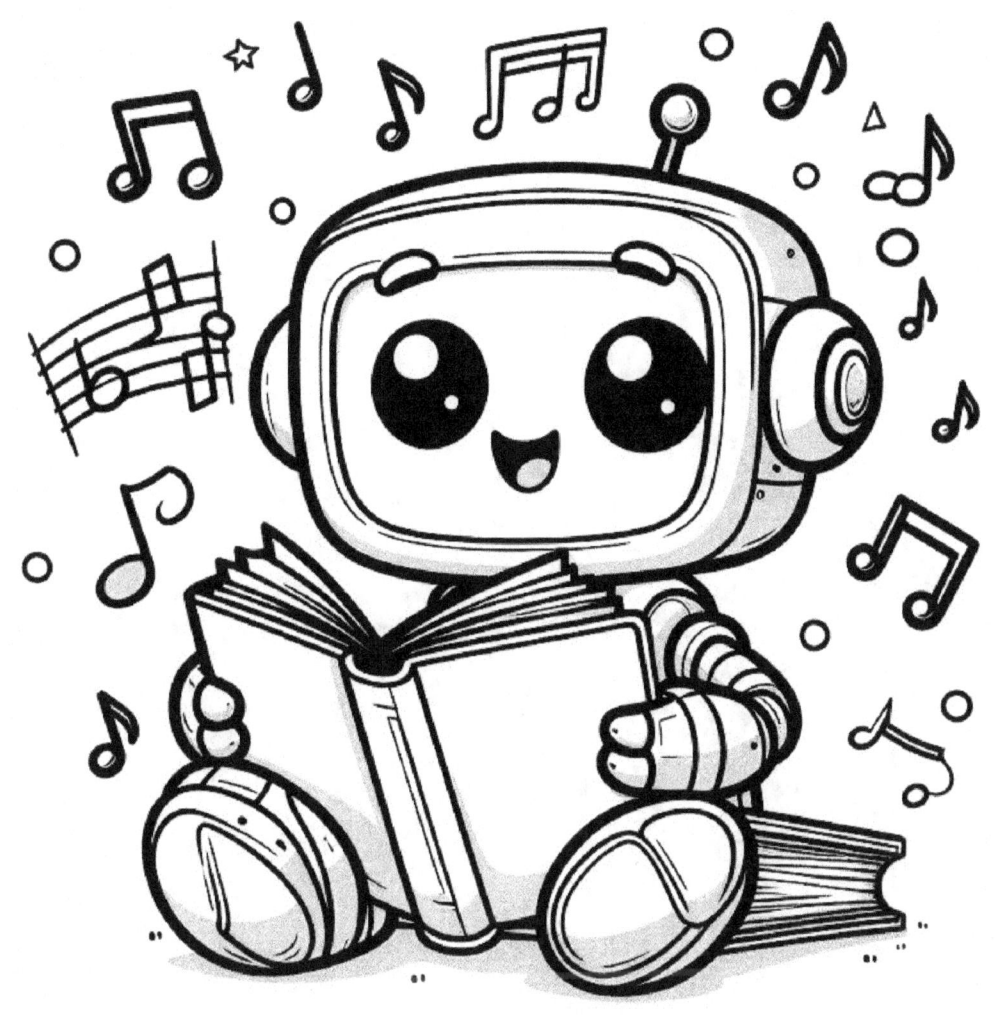

Whenever he heard his favorite song, he would sing it out of tune, which alienated those around him

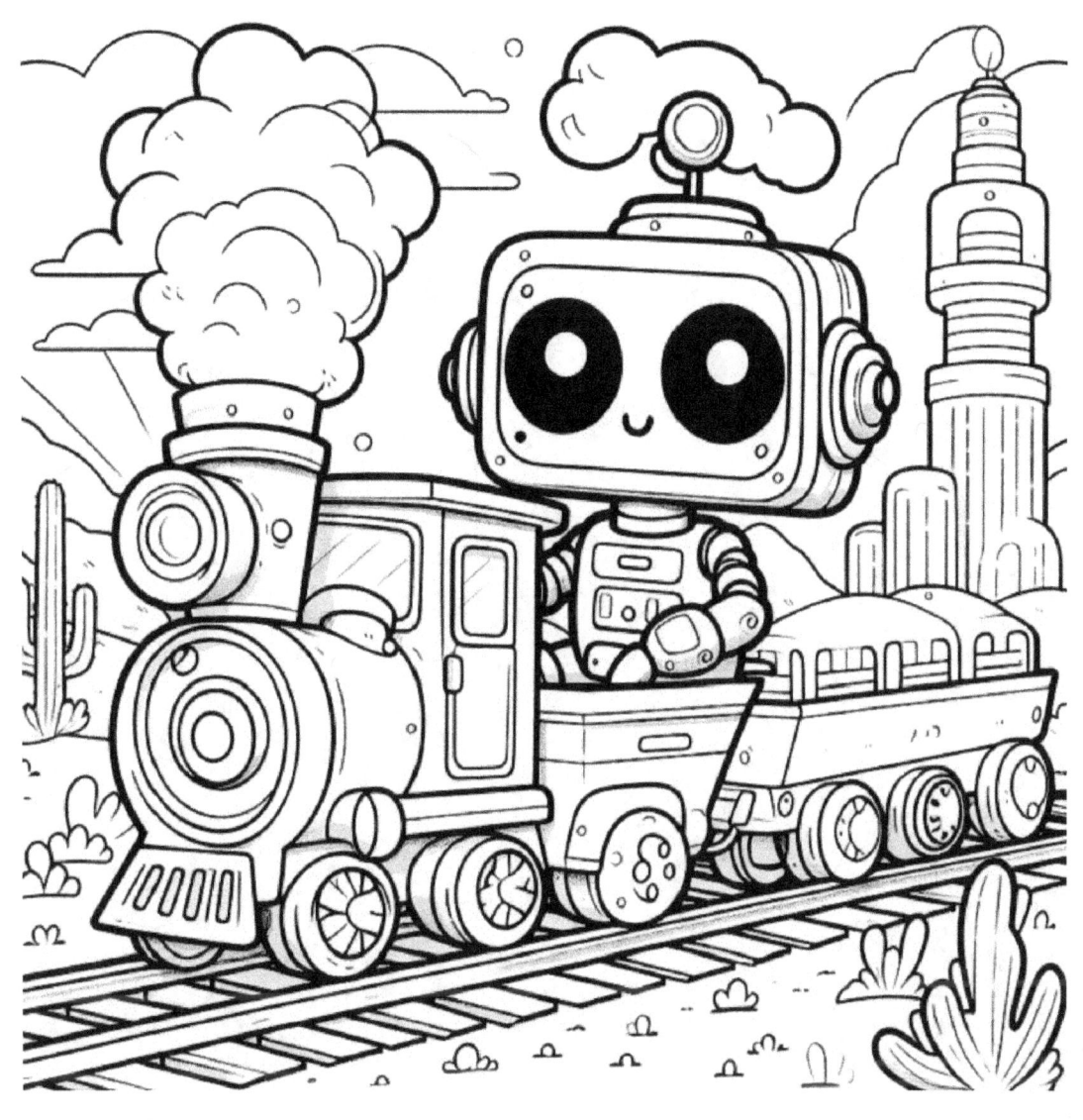

Niti Liky used to ride the little train that connected his town to the sunflower plantation.

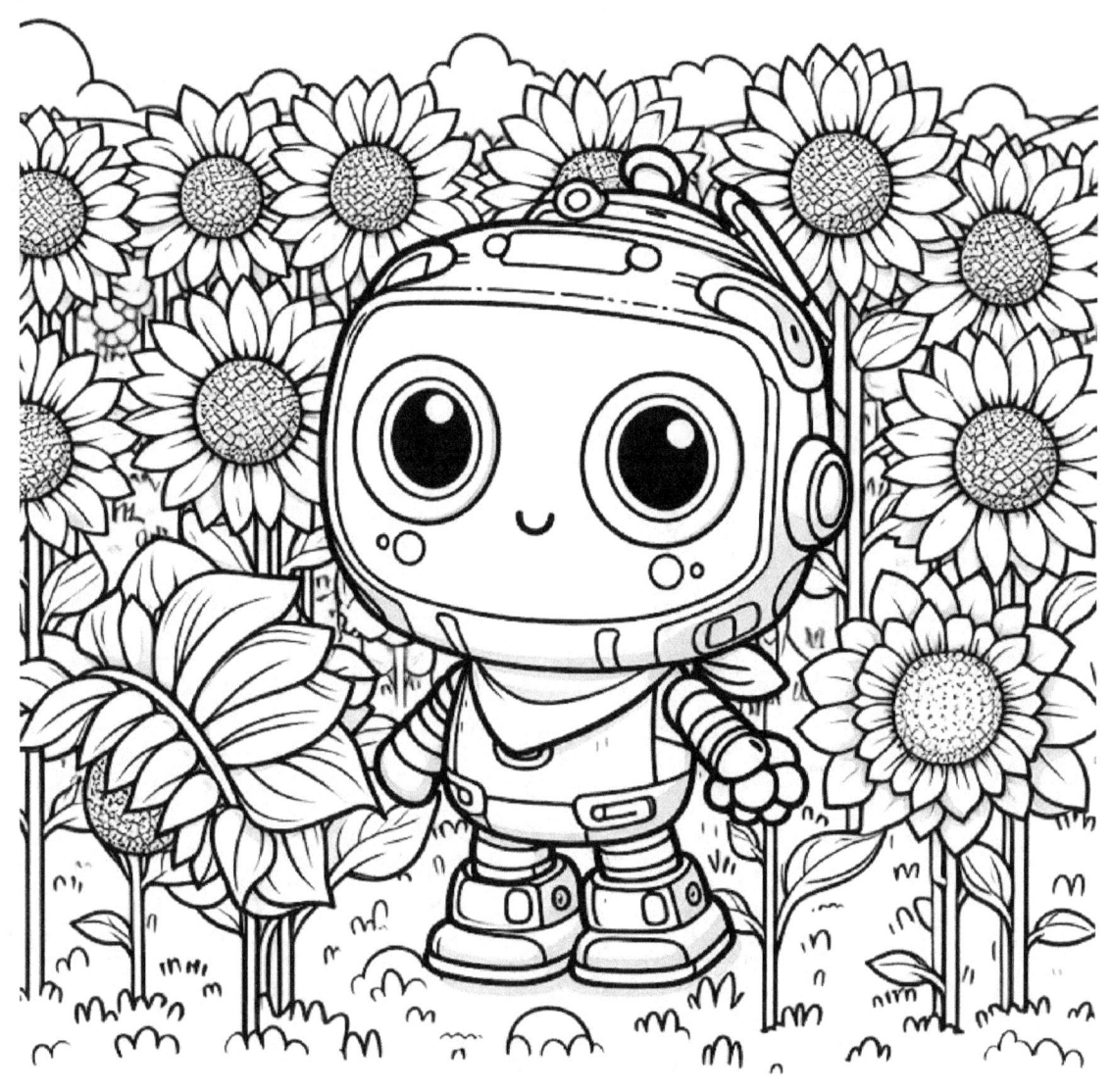

The sunflower plantation was a very beautiful place, full of sunflowers and birds.

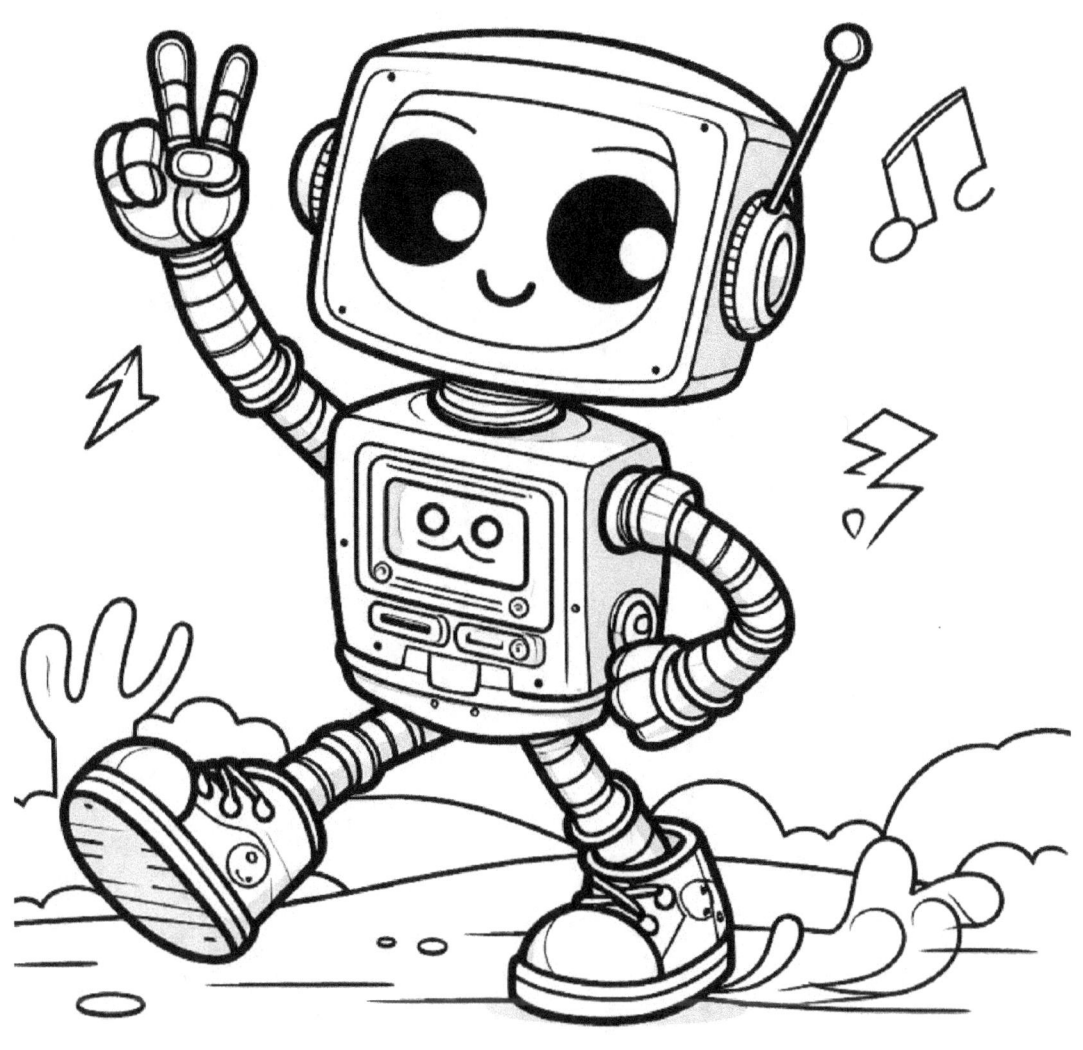

The life of a robot isn't easy: studying, working, taking care of animals, and training in karate.
Would you like to be a little robot?

www.ingramcontent.com/pod-product-compliance
Lightning Source LLC
Chambersburg PA
CBHW082212220526
45470CB00010B/3142